FINANCIAL MARKET MELTDOWN

▼

FINANCIAL MARKET MELTDOWN

▼

Everything You Need to Know to Understand and Survive the Global Credit Crisis

KEVIN MELLYN

PRAEGER
An Imprint of ABC-CLIO, LLC

Santa Barbara, California • Denver, Colorado • Oxford, England

Library of Congress Cataloging-in-Publication Data

Mellyn, Kevin.
   Financial market meltdown : everything you need to know to understand and survive the global credit crisis / Kevin Mellyn.
      p. cm.
   Includes index.
   Also available on the Web as an ebook.
   ISBN 978-0-313-37776-1 (hard copy : alk. paper) –
ISBN 978-0-313-37777-8 (ebook)
   1. Finance–United States–History–21st century. 2. Financial crises–United States–History–21st century. I. Title.
   HB3722.M45 2009
   332.0973–dc22   2009029157

ISBN: 978-0-313-37776-1
EISBN: 978-0-313-37777-8

13   12   11   10   09   1   2   3   4   5

This book is also available on the World Wide Web as an eBook.
Visit www.abc-clio.com for details.

Praeger
An Imprint of ABC-CLIO, LLC

ABC-CLIO, LLC
130 Cremona Drive, P.O. Box 1911
Santa Barbara, California 93116-1911

This book is printed on acid-free paper ∞

Manufactured in the United States of America

To my wife Judy, who has always patiently supported my writing ventures and both typed the handwritten drafts of the text and suggested important changes in direction and tone throughout the project, and to my historian daughter Elizabeth who offered great encouragement and good advice to her dad.

CONTENTS

▼

INTRODUCTION
Money, Markets, Manias, and You

▼

The purpose of this book is to help you understand what is happening in the global financial economy, why it is happening, and what can be done about it. Few people outside the so-called financial services industry even pretend to understand how money and credit really work. Current events show that even the so-called financial professionals understood too little about the basics of money and credit. This is very much a book about the basics of money. It has a single aim: To make the idea of money in all its forms and uses simple and concrete for you, the general reader. Armed with that understanding, you can and should make your own judgments not only about your personal financial best interests but about the best interests of your country and, indeed, the world.

The global financial market crisis that occurred in 2008 unleashed a torrent of words and ideas that few people understand. More to the point, your elected representatives have a very imperfect understanding of what is going on and what can be done about it. What's more, they have a strong interest in making sure that you understand even less than they do. Think *The Wizard of Oz*. The world is not and cannot be run by the *great and the good*. It is too complex to be run by anybody. It is run by millions of people like you who need and want money. As the song in the musical Cabaret has it: "Money makes the world go round." But what if suddenly the music stops?

A financial crisis like the one we are currently living through throws into sharp focus how much we all take for granted the safety and reliability of money itself and by extension the complex machinery that makes it work. Now we all see that the machinery is not working. Since money makes the world go round, this crisis threatens every aspect of daily life, or so it seems. But financial crises have occurred throughout history. The world always muddles through, suffering more or less damage. Money always comes back. So, rather than add more ink on the subject of the causes and cures of today's troubles, this book seeks to demystify the workings of money and the machinery of money at all times and in all places. If successful, the basic ideas in this book will be useful to readers far into the future, if only to allow them to understand the world of money at least as well as the "leaders" who count on our incomprehension. Remember how Dorothy and her friends were all better off when Oz was unmasked?

MONEY

We are ruled by money. We sacrifice our time, our affections, and often our consciences for money. The making and getting of money is the principal business of life for most of us. At the same time, very few people can say what money actually is. Naturally, economists define money, but they do it in a way that nobody outside the priesthood of their profession can understand. That, after all, is what being a professional is all about. People who make a living dealing in money have their own, but no more enlightening, jargon. So, we have "hot money," "smart money," "dumb money" and, of course, "mad money," along with scores of other insider terms peculiar to individual financial markets or institutions.

Financial Tower of Babel

Not only is financial jargon impenetrable to ordinary people, the world of money speaks in many tongues. Bankers do not understand the lingo of the insurance business and vice versa. Stock and bond markets have different languages, as do foreign exchange and commodity markets. Even among English-speaking countries, the same words mean entirely different things. In the United States, corporate equity is called stock while in London it is called shares. Just to make things complicated, the Brits trade shares on the stock exchange and of course, much of what Yanks call "bonds" are in fact "stock" in U.K. English. Add in additional languages, and the fact that every country's history has resulted in a slightly different set of financial institutions and instruments, and the possibility for confusion is vast. This is why even the highest-quality financial journalism, such as that churned out by the *Financial Times* and *The Economist* newspapers in London, is of limited help to even well-educated readers without experience in finance. So, in concrete terms, what is money?

Exchange

Money is whatever you are willing to accept in return for something you have to offer to someone else. If we see a man with a sign around his neck saying "will work for food" then food for him is money. He will accept it in exchange for work. For most people in the world, daily life still operates this way, and, at one point only a few centuries ago, it did for pretty much everyone. People exchanged labor or other services for "stuff" they needed, like food and shelter. Just because people are trading in "stuff"—in other words engaging in "bartering"—does not mean that they are not using money. Stuff that can be traded, including labor or the right to use a plot of land, is a form of money, at least potentially. The problem with "stuff" as money is that it is hard to use beyond a small, closed circle of people. The guy who will work for food may or may not be able to do any work you really need or are willing to pay for. The food you have to offer him may not be what he wants and needs. There is no way to fairly measure the value of the work or the food. Everything comes down to haggling and depends on how hungry the guy is and how much you need the help he can provide. These things are not easy to know. And they change with circumstances.

Markets

There are very few examples of human societies in which people did not trade or "truck" with each other to better themselves. From a practical viewpoint, nobody can be good at everything, and we all only have so much time in the day. So it makes sense to exchange or swap what we have or are good at for what we need. A good trapper is better off trading pelts for food with farmers than he would be trying to both grow food and tend his traps. Since exchanges like this will become routine in any group of people, a rule of thumb will emerge for how much corn a pelt should fetch. This is largely a question of many face-to-face haggling sessions over time that result in an expected, or "customary," "price." Unless someone can set prices through politics or someone holds all the supply of corn or pelts, prices will move up or down with changing circumstances. It will take more pelts to buy the same measure of corn in a bad harvest year. A cold winter might drive up the number of pelts that farmers want.

Prices

We learned about the "law of supply and demand" when we took a basic course in economics. When you find more than two people wanting to exchange or swap the same "stuff," you have a market in that "stuff." More to the point, unless somebody for some reason actively stops it from happening, the market will decide what prices should be for each kind of stuff. As the economists put it, markets do something call "price discovery." They allow people to find out what something is worth. The trapper comes out of the woods with his pelts and learns or "discovers" how much corn they will fetch, not by haggling with one farmer, but by learning what all farmers are willing to give him. This will mean he needs to bring his stuff to a market. This might be in a village that is conveniently located near both farms and woods. It might occur at an open-air fair that meets from time to time. The larger and more frequently the market between trappers and farmers happens, the more trades will happen. These trades will set the "price" between pelts and corn after anyone who wants to swap one for the other has done so. This is how markets set prices. The markets "clear," as economists put it, when all the stuff brought to a market gets exchanged or swapped, so nobody wanting corn is still holding out for more pelts and vice versa. This establishes what corn is worth in terms of pelts and what pelts are worth in terms of corn.

Commodity Money

The question not solved by this system is, what are corn and pelts worth relative to *other* "stuff"? Usually, this problem gets solved by having one type of stuff that acts as the central swaping good for all other goods and services. This centralization of value is the basic function of "money." However, exactly what one should use as money is not obvious. Everything could be traded and priced in terms of corn, for example, and indeed grain has been used in this way and in places no doubt still is. However, grain is bulky, perishable, comes in many types and qualities, and can be produced in many places. It is relatively easy to increase its supply, thus reducing its value in terms of other stuff. It therefore makes poor money even if markets for grain that are very large and fair develop. Stuff that cannot be made in many places, comes from far away, and is something of a luxury, makes a better money, though still not the best. The ancient world of the Mediterranean used olive oil and wine as a sort of money. These products were far more compact and harder to produce than grain, although they were still relatively bulky. Even today many rich people invest in kinds of fine wine for which there is a well-established global market.

MONEY AND MARKETS

For money to be really useful, it needs to be something truly useless. Instead of swapping stuff for stuff, people need to find something that can be swapped for any kind of stuff that they need. This is, in economist speak, a "medium of exchange." In effect, one type of stuff comes to occupy the middle point of any and all swaps. Instead of trading my pelts for corn, I trade them for a quantity of stuff that I cannot eat but that anyone with food to sell me will accept in return. Note the word *sell*. Instead of swapping stuff, now everyone sells what they have for one type of stuff: Money. For most people, what they have to sell is themselves. We trade work for money, either by selling what we produce or simply doing work for someone willing to pay us money. Money allows us to *buy* anything offered for sale at a price. We don't have to spend our time bartering for everything we need, or worse making everything we need ourselves. Instead we can focus on doing the things that, given our circumstances, offer us the best return in money. That is why you don't see $800-an-hour lawyers mowing their own lawns.

Money allows us to specialize, and thus makes us better at what we do. Bond traders don't fix their cars, and BMW mechanics don't trade bonds. In any case, swapping stuff for money rather than stuff for stuff is a lot more convenient for both buyers and sellers. It also allows us to store up buying power for the future, what we call savings, because money is not something we have to consume. Above all, money is a way of keeping score in markets. Everything has a price that can be expressed in units of money, so we know how much a gallon of gasoline is worth relative to a gallon of milk. We don't have to do a swap to find this out. The market—all the buyers and all the sellers—will at the end of the day settle on a price for everything. Markets are not perfect, and buyers or sellers can have "unfair advantages" in terms of information and power. However, nobody has ever come up with a better way of "discovering" prices, which is the key to all buying and selling.

Acceptance

So we know that something that is in itself useless (or nearly so) that everyone will swap their stuff for is the key quality of money. The big idea behind this is something called "acceptance." If people come to accept something as money, it becomes money. For example, cowrie shells in West Africa were once universally accepted as money. People bought and sold goods and labor through the medium of cowrie shells. They were durable, easy to carry, and in limited supply outside the coastal areas. This made them convenient. When the British ruled much of West Africa, the kind of paper money and coins we are familiar with were used in the cities, but banks had to convert this Western money to cowrie shells in rural districts. Western notes and coins had no local acceptance, so if African farmers sold their crops in return for such money, they needed to turn it into real money—cowrie shells.

GOLD

In the West, gold has been used as money for thousands of years because of its almost universal acceptance across cultures. While certainly decorative, gold has little "use value" as a metal. At any given time, the amount of gold used for money has exceeded that used for luxury goods. The same also used to be true for silver, another relatively soft and shiny metal of limited practical use. The key to using both gold and silver as money was that their supply was always very limited relative to market demand for them. This does not explain why one type of stuff called gold became, and for a long time remained, a nearly universally accepted type of money. Very high market prices for gold relative to other stuff must have helped though. People were willing to swap a lot of stuff, including things like land and power, for small physical amounts of gold. This meant that a valuable quantity of gold was relatively easy to store and carry; a little gold could buy a lot. And, over very long periods of time, it held its value relative to other stuff. However, the fact that gold turned out to be the stuff most of the world used as the standard for money came down to acceptance.

TOP DOWN AND BOTTOM UP

Of course, acceptance doesn't just happen on its own. Something can become accepted as money "bottom-up" through an increase of trust based on the experience of individuals over time. This is probably how we got both gold and cowrie shells as money. It is certainly how we got plastic cards and, earlier, checks as the functional equivalents of money. The mother of all battles for acceptance, however, was no doubt the widespread replacement of "hard money"—gold and silver coin—with "paper money" issued by banks. Today, we all think of paper currency as "real" money, something that is of value even if the banks go bust. Getting us to that point took about two centuries, and the injection of "top down" government power. Governments have a trump card when it comes to acceptance: They can declare that a form of money is "legal tender," which means that you by law have to accept it as a form of payment. They are also in a unique position to dictate what forms of payment they themselves will accept as payment for taxes. In fact, the money we mostly think of as cash today—coins and bills—owe at least as much to "top down" power as they do to "bottom up" market development. Coins started out as a means of making life easier for governments. Three thousand years ago, governments were mainly concerned with paying their soldiers. This could be done by collecting taxes in the form of agricultural produce and paying armies out of the royal storehouses. For a long time, this is precisely what went on in most of the ancient world. Coins of uniform metallic content and design were introduced in Lydia (part of today's Turkey) around 600 BC. The acceptance problem was solved because the king would only accept the coins he produced in payment of taxes. It was up to the tax payer to sell his stuff in return for coin. Since the king paid his troops and suppliers in coin, acceptance and the amount of coin in circulation grew rapidly. Striking coins became, and for centuries remained, a key aspect of asserting power in a kingdom or an empire. "The coin of the realm" was the basis of value, the bedrock of money, even if a lot of barter still went on in everyday life.

Even today, coins continue to jingle in our purses and make holes in our pockets. The difference is that today coins have no real value as "stuff." During the centuries before the 1930s, coins of high value were minted out of real gold and real silver, so-called "precious metals." Even small denominations contained real nickel, copper, and bronze. They had some intrinsic value as "stuff." Indeed, governments were sometimes caught "debasing the currency," that is, diluting the gold and silver content of coinage with cheap base metals. Crooks "shaved" coins, filing a little gold or silver off the edges. Governments took a dim view of this, treating it as a form of treason and subject to very grisly penalties.

There are two lessons here. One, no basic form of money introduced over the millennia has ever entirely gone out of use. We still use coins in everyday life, and some of us even buy gold coins as an "investment." Second, even if the form of money remains constant, the underlying market reality can change completely. Coins that were once made of very valuable and scarce "stuff" are now stamped out of cheap industrial alloy. Paper money before the 1930s could be exchanged by the holder for gold and silver coin. Now they give the holder no legal claim to actual valuable stuff. Why, then, is the money we use worth anything at all?

CREDIT

This brings us to the second key point: Using money is an act of faith. Every time we accept a coin, we believe it to have the value that is marked on it. We believe this partially because we have to—"legal tender" means we have to accept government-made money. But no one thinks about it that way. Our act of faith is based on habit and on what other people believe. We grew up learning that cheap metal disks and bits of printed paper were a special, really valuable kind of "stuff." And because everyone else believes the same thing, this "stuff" really is special. The Latin verb for "to believe" or "to trust" is "credere." That is where the word "credit" comes from, "creditum" or trust.

Credit is where money and markets come together. Credit is the very heart of economic life and forms the central theme of this book. When we say that a government, a company, or an individual has "good credit," we mean that they keep their word. We believe that we can trust them to make good on their promises. I will give a co-worker a few dollars to buy lunch because I know them and trust them to pay me back. Banks make similar credit decisions about their customers all the time. So do companies buying and selling between each other. And, ultimately, banks make credit decisions about each other.

The question at the heart of credit is always the same: If "X" promises to pay me a certain sum of money by a certain time, do I really believe they will do so? If I believe that they actually want to pay me, can I believe "X" will be able to keep their word at the time the money is due? This means that I have to believe that "X" will actually have the money they owe me at a future date. We know that bad things happen all the time, and we can't really predict future events, so this is always a bet rather than a certainty. So is my belief that "X" will want to keep their word. We know that not everyone is perfectly honest, and we cannot be sure what circumstances will tempt "X" to break their promise, especially if they think they can get away with it. Again, this cannot be predicted with certainty. Yet we make bets of this kind all the time. Ultimately, the bets of millions upon millions of us add up to a bottom-up vote that we believe that "X" can and will keep their promises to pay. "X" can be the government, banks, businesses, or ordinary people. The point is that the belief that "X" will keep their promises makes those promises themselves a special kind of money, what is called credit.

Like the special value we attach to bits of paper and cheap metal disks, credit is entirely an act of faith. Only it is not just faith in the government but also in each other. People, companies, banks, and even governments all have better or worse credit based on the balance between faith and doubt about how they can and will keep their promises. To a degree, this balance depends on information, especially our experience and observations about past behavior. But it is also a question of the balance between hope and fear of the future. When we are optimistic about the future, we are far more likely to use credit. And in good times, lenders of all kinds are eager to give us credit. Invitations to borrow money tumble through our mail boxes whether we need credit or not. However, as we now know all too well from the events of 2008, optimism can turn to panic on a dime. Fear about the future can make credit disappear overnight. And when fear takes hold, restoring both the appetite for using credit and the willingness to provide credit can be a long and painful process. Credit is both a powerful and a delicate thing.

Credit as Money

The key point is that though it is based on little but faith and is subject to our collective mood swings, credit is the most important form of money in the world. It is a kind of "stuff" that can be traded for other "stuff" in the market. In fact, there is a special market for credit itself in which thousands of banks and other borrowers and lenders trade around the world and around the clock. Credit markets are concrete and tangible things, supported by hundreds of thousands of workers in thousands of offices, around the globe. They have laws, practices, and customs, like any market. Central to this book is the idea that our understanding of the global credit market can be made as real and concrete to the reader as the market where they buy their groceries.

Manias

The great advantage and virtue of credit money over all other forms of "stuff" that can and have been used for money is that it has no physical existence. It really is "money of the mind." This means that a great deal of credit money can be created out of very little concrete stuff. It is incredibly elastic. When there are good and sound uses for money—a new technology or a new market to be financed, or a national emergency like a war—credit can be expanded to the point that optimism, or as it is commonly called "confidence," will permit. Everyone can borrow because everyone will lend.

Panics

Like any elastic material, however, credit can snap and whip back on its users. The force of any backlash that can occur is directly proportional to the degree to which the credit system has been stretched in the first place. As was noted above, faith largely depends on everyone believing in the same thing. For example, if everyone believes that dot.com companies that never earned a dime of revenue are worth more than many of the largest industrial corporations, then it is in fact true. Markets simply record judgments, acts of faith, about what stuff is worth. If these companies can sell stock at sky-high prices, it is because everyone believes those companies will be worth more tomorrow. As the prices rise, people who own stock feel richer. On paper, they are richer. They spend more. They borrow more. They buy more stock. If, however, the enchantment is broken, the process is thrown into reverse. Suddenly nobody believes that prices will rise, so everyone tries to get out while they can. Paper fortunes evaporate. Debts can't be paid. Credit dries up.

SWINGS AND ROUNDABOUTS

This pattern of people swinging from wild optimism—mania is the classic term—to flat out panic—another classic term—is as old as time. Man is a social animal and runs in herds. An economy based on "hard" money like gold or other commodities has less "stretch" on the way up or on the way down. Manias and panics are still possible, and history records many. However, an economy based almost entirely on credit money is subject to really violent cycles of over-expansion followed by over-contraction of borrowing and lending. The better the "machinery" of the credit market works in terms of how much lending can be extended to how many people, the more the cycle is likely to overshoot on the way up and on the way down.

Access to credit cuts both ways. There are economies and cultures that make it very hard if not impossible for most people and businesses to get any credit. In fact, most of the world can be described in these terms. They may, to an extent, avoid the whipsaws of a dynamic and open credit system. However, people in these places pay a big price for stability.

Boom and bust, mania and panic, can be very destructive and wasteful. They are very frightening on the way down. But risk and reward are stubbornly joined at the hip. High-velocity financial systems powered by credit money inevitably blow up from time to time. They do this for reasons rooted not in greed and corruption, as some may believe, but in common human nature. Markets are subject to boom and bust because people swing between unwarranted optimism and excessive fear. Always have, always will.

Credit-driven financial markets have, on the other hand, proved to be incredibly effective in creating new industries, new jobs, and over time much higher living standards where they have been free to work. It would be nice if smart people could figure out a way to take out the potential for destruction in credit money without loss of these great benefits. This book will explain why the great and good in government and finance have not and cannot in fact do so. Until the global financial market meltdown of 2008 fell upon us, "the powers that be" in government and finance worldwide actually believed that they had domesticated the beast that now threatens our jobs and homes. Now we know better.

YOU

This book is really less about money and credit than it is about you. If we succeed in what we set out to do in this book, we will have given you a framework for understanding the world of money and credit. Your understanding will not make you rich. But it should make you more independent and confident in your decisions concerning money and finance.

The basic framework and the order in which describe this world of money are based on the work of Walter Bagehot, a great English writer on banking and much else, who lived over a century ago. As a banker and a journalist, he lived through a terrible financial panic and an economic depression that lasted for many years. Many of his friends who didn't understand banking asked him to help them understand what was happening. So he wrote a book for them. His great aim was to make the money market, then, as now, a great abstraction and mystery to most people, as concrete and real as possible. Today's far more complex financial world still lends itself to Bagehot's descriptive approach. The global credit market is an abstraction, but real people and real institutions work in it. Please remember though that this book is very much one man's view, and it makes no claim of getting all the details right.

1

▼

A TOUR OF THE FINANCIAL WORLD AND ITS INHABITANTS

THE TWO ECONOMIES

Most of us live in the "real economy." We get up and go to work in order to get paid. We are paid in something called money. We don't need to understand what money is or how it works. We spend it. We pay taxes. We buy stuff we need or at least want. We pay bills. Some of us save or invest what we don't spend, and many of us borrow to spend more than we earn. Most of us don't give a thought to how the money we use to buy stuff of that we save or borrow really works as long as it *does* work. Now though, we are suddenly told by the politicians and "experts" that the "global financial system" has frozen up. But what does that really mean in concrete terms? And, how do we fix it?

This is too big a question for people who live in the "real economy" to leave to "experts" and political "leaders." The purpose of this chapter is to make the "financial economy" as concrete and understandable as the "real economy" of our everyday lives.

This distinction between the "real economy" and "financial economy" is not to be confused with the glib contrast between "Main Street" and "Wall Street" as used by political types. That is totally false, even a dishonest, distinction. The real economy is the basis of the financial economy. No work, no income, no spending and borrowing equals no financial economy. However, on the other hand, the financial economy is the lifeblood of the real economy. No payment system (think checks and credit cards), no credit, no investment equals no real economy, or at least a very poor one. Rich, dynamic countries with high living standards depend a lot more on their financial economies to power their real economies than backward countries. The two economies feed each other.

Handle with Care

At the same time, the financial economy is as delicate as it is powerful. When it is working well, the financial economy provides the real economy with high-octane credit money that speeds progress and raises living standards. Good things like creation of more jobs happen in the real economy that couldn't happen otherwise. When it is working too well, however, people forget how extremely delicate it really is. They get confident, even cocky, and begin to push their luck. It only takes a little bad judgment to blow up the financial economy. High-octane, easy credit is volatile. When it blows, the financial economy can quickly drag the real economy down in flames with it. We are living through just such an explosion and fire right now. As we have said, these things we call "panics" happen on a pretty regular basis.

What makes the global financial crisis that exploded in 2008 historically unique is the unprecedented scale that the financial economy has recently assumed relative to the real economy. The last time that the world was thrown into a downward spiral by the collapse of the financial system was the 1930s. Since then, many individual countries have suffered financial meltdowns, but this time the whole world financial system has gone into the tank at the same time. The big difference between the 1930s and now is that, back then, the economy was driven by the manufacturing industry, not finance. Today, we are living in a world built upon and driven by finance, in places like New York City and London, and little else. This means that when a politician says we are facing the worst crisis in 80 years, he doesn't know what he is talking about—we are facing something unprecedented. The numbers are sobering.

In 1946, the first full post-war year, the U.S. economy was the largest in the world, producing over $200 billion in national income. The "financial economy" that provided credit money and investment funds for their "real economy" was substantial, some $350 billion in outstanding (that is, owed and payable in the future) debt. However, households only owed a tenth of this—$35 billion—and businesses of all types only accounted for $56 billion more. The federal government owed the vast majority of the outstanding debt, some $230 billion. That was a direct result of the cost of fighting the largest war in history.

THE FINANCE TAIL WAGS THE ECONOMIC DOG

Flash forward 60 years to 2006. National income has exceeded $13 trillion, multiplying 65 times in constant dollars (that is, not adjusting for the "real" value of a buck). However, outstanding credit has exploded to over $45 trillion, nearly 3 times the total output of the U.S. economy. This is an increase of 130 times in constant dollars. In other words, the financial economy, as measured by credit outstanding, has grown twice as fast as the real economy over a 60-year period. However, this was not a continuous, straight-line sort of thing. Total credit outstanding was a bit less than $20 trillion in 1996, about 2 times the national output. The extra $25 trillion was all borrowed over the next 10 years. Meanwhile, total national output only rose a bit over $5 trillion for the decade.

In other words, the real economy dog was increasingly being wagged by the credit tail. Growth was impressive in the "real economy" despite shocks like the collapse of dot.com stocks, corporate scandals like Enron, and the attacks of 9/11. However, it took more and more in credit dollars to produce an extra dollar of economic output. For example, between 2005 and 2007, the United States added almost $1.4 trillion in output. However, debt outstanding went up by $8.6 trillion over the same two years. In other words, the U.S. economy was taking on about six dollars of debt for every extra dollar of income. And, like an addict needing a fix, the required debt dose kept on rising. In stark contrast, the post-war economic boom saw U.S. national output triple between 1946 and 1956 while outstanding debt only went up by about three quarters. In the 1950s, we grew the economy by making stuff but more recently we have grown the economy by borrowing money. In other words, the United States has become a credit-driven economy to a degree not seen before in all of history.

Now, this is not in and of itself a bad thing. The United States *was* growing faster than other "developed" economies such as Japan and the European Union as its financial economy outstripped its real economy. It was creating vastly more new jobs and new companies than these more financially conservative countries. To many, at home and abroad, the U.S. financial-driven economy looked like the best model for the world to follow. In fact, a lot of what is called "globalization"—a very loaded and slippery term—is little more than the spread of the U.S. model of a finance-driven economy around the world. This system was a game anyone could play, at least up to a point. In fact, the world had seen this particular movie before, just with a somewhat different cast. Victorian Britain was the world's first finance-driven economy. Writing in 1873, our friend Walter Bagehot noted that England differed from other countries in the sheer quantity of what he called "borrowable money" that was made available by the London money market. The English businessman was in the habit of "constant and chronic borrowing" and could to a unique degree "trade on borrowed capital" simply because money could be had from the market for any good purpose.

THE AGE OF LEVERAGE

This is exactly where the vast "financial economy" of the United States stood on the eve of the current disastrous snap-back of the credit elastic. Money could be had cheaply until the summer of 2007, for any purpose or no purpose at all. The huge American financial economy of 2007 could be described exactly as Bagehot summed up the "great London loan pool" of his time: "The greatest combination of economic *power* and economic *delicacy* the world had ever seen."

The power of borrowed money is obvious and can be summed up in an ugly word unknown to Bagehot's time: *Leverage.* Just as a physical lever multiplies physical force, financial leverage multiplies what can be done with money. If I use a thousand dollars of my own money to buy something I can sell for two thousand dollars, I can double my money. But if I can use my one thousand dollars to borrow ten thousand dollars, the same trade fetches ten times the money. The return on my own money, even after I pay the lender for use of his money, is many times what I could earn trading on my own "capital," the name for the money that I really own. The power, and therefore attractiveness, of leverage is obvious.

The "delicacy" part of Bagehot's quote is less obviously defined and more easily overlooked. As we noted in the introduction, using credit money is an act of faith based largely on group psychology, which can turn on a dime. A financial economy that allows, or, worse, encourages too much borrowing and leverage, is almost bound to blow up. But a lack of credit and financial leverage is very bad too. Countries that allow very limited access to banking and credit to most people and businesses are much poorer than those where credit is widely available.

What Bagehot really meant by "delicacy" is not that credit is dangerous as such. The delicacy refers to a fine balance that needs to be maintained between risk and reward, fear and greed. Now, classical economic theory would tell us that this delicate balance can be maintained by rational people acting in their own prudent and best interest. Bagehot, who was a free-market defender and banker himself, did not believe this for a second. Neither should we. In his own day, he had lived through enough panics to sense that the sheer scale of the British financial economy and its rapid growth were making "accidents" more frequent and damaging to the real economy. The same goes for the U.S. financial economy, in spades. Maintaining the delicate balance in his day required active management because "money will not manage itself," in his famous phrase. He was right. The failure of London's premier financial house in 1873 set off a panic that marked the start of a worldwide Great Depression that lasted until 1894.

THE ECOLOGY OF FINANCE

To fully appreciate both the vast power and the extreme delicacy of the financial economy, we need a concrete notion of how it works in normal times. Here, it will help to avoid mechanical descriptions and terms that writers on finance are prone to use. There is no "financial

system" that smart people purposefully designed and built to manufacture and circulate credit money. Things are a lot messier than that.
Nobody designed anything, and nobody is really in charge. Instead,
the financial system we have is the result of evolutionary accidents. It
is more like an ecology in which various animals are more or less in
balance with each other most of the time, eating or being eaten, until
there is a "shock" like a wildfire or stampede. Some critters get killed,
some get stronger, and things settle down in a new balance. Think of
a *Nature Channel* show about a jungle or savannah and its inhabitants
and how they live. The financial economy is a lot more like a food
chain than an electric power grid.

THE BOTTOM OF THE FOOD CHAIN

At the bottom of the food chain is the creature that all the other
inhabitants feed off. You, the average household, feed all the critters
in the economic jungle we live in. The household sector in any
advanced country powers the "real economy," accounting for the vast
majority of spending, savings, and wealth. Take the United States, for
example. According to our official "national accounts" published by
the Federal Reserve each quarter, U.S. households had $78 trillion in
assets in the summer of 2007 just before the financial crisis. By contrast, households owed $14 trillion dollars, leaving them with a net
worth—the value of their assets after subtracting all debt owed—of
$64 trillion. That's *trillion*, as in 1000 billion. To put this enormous
wealth in perspective, the total output of the U.S. economy—what
the economists call GDP or gross domestic product—was only about
$13 trillion. In fact, world GDP was only about $45 trillion or so in
2007.

This vast accumulated wealth of households fell into two large
buckets: First, tangible assets of $28 trillion, including over $21 trillion in real estate and $4 trillion in durable goods like cars; and sec-
ond, financial assets of $50 trillion. Of these, only about $7 trillion
was "money in the bank" such as in checking and savings accounts or
money market funds. Most household financial assets are what are
called "market instruments." These will be described in detail in the
next chapter, but in general, a market instrument is either an IOU for
borrowed money or an ownership share in a corporation. In other

words, what we know as bonds and stocks. Households owned abut $4 trillion in bonds of various types and $15 trillion in stock, about a third of it through mutual funds. Indirectly, pension funds and insurance companies had comparable holdings to back up promises to households.

This pile of financial assets was vastly in excess of any money that households owed, about $13 trillion in the summer of 2007. However, looking at the balance sheet of the whole population masks a crucial truth. Both the wealth, in the form of both tangible and financial assets, and the debt, $10.5 trillion of it mortgages and the rest in consumer credit, including a trillion on credit cards, were very unevenly spread. *All* American households as a group have lots of financial wealth even now, even after the big decline in the stock market. However, most of this wealth is concentrated in the top-earning households. *All* American households as a group still have nearly $8.5 trillion in equity in their houses despite the sharp and continuing fall in home prices. But this equity is concentrated in the half of all households who own their houses outright or have paid down their mortgages to a large extent. With the fall in house prices knocking over $2 trillion off the household equity in homes, millions of families owe more on their mortgages than their houses are worth.

Viewed this way, the level of consumer debt on the household balance sheet looks a lot more alarming, especially when you compare it to the amount of income that households actually receive—about $8 trillion. Income itself is highly concentrated, with about half of it going to the top 10%, and 23% of income to the top 1% of all U.S. households. In fact, average household incomes have been more or less flat for decades, for a variety of reasons. As a result, many U.S. households have increasingly relied on credit as a substitute for income to maintain their lifestyles. They have been doing this for two decades. Now, with the crisis, they suddenly can't. Credit has disappeared overnight. This is the meat of our economic crisis. Much ink has already been spilled over what caused this to happen. There are also lots of ideas about how to get credit flowing again. These discussions overlook two obvious questions though: How was so much financial wealth amassed by households in the first place? How were so many of them able to accumulate so much personal debt? In other words, the question that is really enlightening to ask isn't why things went wrong, but how did this go on for so long without a major blow-up? For the real answers to these questions, we need to take a look at all the financial economy creatures that live off the bottom feeders, the households and their balance sheets.

THE BANKS

In the financial jungle, all the inhabitants are trying to get a small slice of the huge monetary beast that we just described. Remember, the household balance sheet is just a snapshot of a river of money flowing into and out of the financial accounts held by 120 million or so households and several million small businesses. If you have an average monthly bank balance of $1000, that doesn't mean that you only make and spend $1000 each month. Your total deposits and payments could be several times as much. So, as big as the household balance sheet is, the flows of money it sits in the middle of are much, much larger. And, although it is by far the biggest beast in the money river, the household balance sheet is very slow moving compared with those of banks and businesses. If a household turns over its checking account average balance several times a month, businesses often turn their balances over several times a week, especially financial businesses. Households get and spend money, but businesses churn through money at a much faster rate.

Now remember that the money we are talking about has no physical existence. It is purely money of the mind. However, it is held inside real-world, tangible institutions that own real estate and computers and employ real human beings. The government calls these things "depository institutions" but we all know them as "banks." We tend to think of banks as businesses that lend money. This is simply wrong. Anyone can lend money. Stores and auto makers offer credit, and companies give "trade credit" to each other all the time. We lend our friends and family money from time to time. What makes a bank special is *not* that it lends money, but that it "takes deposits" from the public. When money was still physical stuff—gold and silver—"deposit taking" amounted to safe-keeping. Banks used to have vaults filled with coin. Now, they store something called "deposit money." Deposit money is the water in the river that flows into and out of the household balance sheet and all the other balance sheets in the U.S.

economy and all other economies worldwide. Deposit money is one of the great inventions of human ingenuity, but it is poorly understood by the billions of people who take its wonders for granted.

Deposit Money

It works like this: When you get paid by check, your employer is not giving you anything of intrinsic value. He is giving you an IOU payable by his bank. The check itself is merely a letter telling his bank to pay some amount of "deposit money" from his account to the person to whom the check is payable. Your employer's deposit money is no more than a number, called the "balance," that is recorded in an account they hold at a bank.

In the time of Charles Dickens, an early sort of bank was called a "counting house." They held accounts for merchants in their ledgers; big paper sheets that indicated how much people owed and were owed. A modern bank is still basically a counting house, but instead of Bob Cratchit and his pen, today, the ledgers are kept as computer records. Otherwise, we still have accounts that the bank holds and operates for its customers. The "operations" they perform are for the most part simply updating those account balances every time money is *received* for a customer and added to his or her account balance—a *credit* to the account—or *paid* by the customers to someone else—a *debit* to the account. Credit and debit are very old terms, from the "credito" and "debito" of early bankers in twelfth century Italy. Deposit money is no more than the sum, the bank balance, left over when all the daily credits and debits are added up for an account. This is the basic "work" banks do for customers, and it hasn't changed for 900 years. All computers have done is speed it up and reduce human error. In principle, anyone could run a bank on a laptop computer with a spreadsheet program.

Follow the Money

Now, let's follow your paycheck. Once you have your hands on it, there are several ways you can turn your employer's deposit money into something you can actually use to buy stuff or pay bills. First, you could "cash" the check. This amounts to selling your claim on your employer's deposit money in return for government-issued "legal tender." This can make sense because by law everyone *has* to accept the scraps of paper and stamped metal discs manufactured by the government as payment. Nobody *has* to accept a check. It is not legal tender. It is simply a claim on deposit money that may or may not exist. However, a check is a "negotiable instrument," meaning that it (and more importantly the claim to money that it represents) can be bought and sold or simply assigned—that is "endorsed"—between people. That fact is what allows you to "cash" your check. When you do so, the bank or check-cashing business is actually buying your claim on deposit money in a bank. They are doing so at their own risk, for there is always the chance the account will not be open or have enough of a balance to pay the check. This is why cashing checks is seldom free and often quite expensive.

Check Collection

The second thing you could do with your paycheck is to "deposit" it in a bank account. This can be more complicated than it sounds. Unless you and your employer have accounts in the same bank, in which case the bank will just credit your account and debit your employers in its computer ledgers, your paycheck will need to be "collected." In other words, your deposit will be credited to your account but not as "available" funds on the day of deposit. "Available funds" is bank-speak for deposit money you can immediately use to make payment to others or to draw out of the bank as cash. Historically, in a big country like the United States, with thousands of different banks, check collection was a big deal, and restricting the availability of deposited checks was simple caution. When the bank credits your deposited check, its takes on the risk that the money is really in the account the check is "drawn" on—another old time banker's term, dating back centuries—or indeed that the account is still open. The bank itself does not have the money on its books until it can "present" the check to the bank holding the account on which it is drawn and get paid. That bank could easily be in a distant state.

The bank holding your employer's account has two choices when the check is presented for payment. It can pay the "item"—another bank-speak term mainly used for checks—or it can return the item for a number of standard causes, including lack of funds or lack of proper signatures. "Paying the item" usually amounts to crediting the presenting bank for the deposit money involved on the books of a bank where they both maintain accounts. For example, the regional Federal Reserve banks hold accounts for thousands of commercial banks. So do so-called correspondent banks, large banks in big cities that do a lot of business for other banks including check collection. Sometimes, the banks involved will hold accounts for each other, and the collecting bank will simply be informed—"advised" in bank-speak—that the money has been credited to its account. Many times collection and payments of checks pass through many banks during this process.

Bouncing Checks

For the most part, the check-collection system works very well. About 28 billion checks were paid in 2007, not counting the "on-us" checks in which both accounts are held in the same bank. However, when a check is *not* paid—the old fashioned bank-speak is "dishonored," most people just say "bounced"—things can get very messy. It has to be sent back to the bank it was first deposited in through the same chain of banks that it passed through on the way to be presented. Ultimately, when the bank holding your deposit account gets a bounced check back, it can decide to try to collect it yet again or just give it back to you, deducting the amount from your balance.

All of these mechanics of holding and operating deposit money accounts sounds like it would be a lot of work. However, electronic technology has made things a lot more efficient. Instead of giving you a check, your employer could sign you up for something called direct deposit. This would allow your pay to be sent to your account as a credit transfer directly from your employers account to yours through something called the ACH or Automated Clearing House. If you do home banking on your computer, your bank pays many, if not most, of your bills through the ACH. ATMs allow you to get cash (in reality, turn your deposit money into government banknotes) without writing a check. Payment cards that allow payments to be cleared and settled in special electronic networks have made a big dent in the number of checks we use to pay for stuff in stores. Even the check collection process itself has become increasingly a matter of stripping off and exchanging payment information electronically rather than with paper. Even so, all the methods customers can use to make and receive payment using their deposit-money accounts represent a lot of work and expense for banks. In fact, these costs account, directly or indirectly, for the bulk of operating expenses of most banks.

The Payments System

The technical term for all the methods for moving around deposit money between those who buy stuff—"payors" in bank-speak—and those who are paid for stuff—"payees" in bank-speak—is "the payments system." Without an effective, reliable payments system that makes deposit money usable in daily life, nobody would use it at all. So, banking is really the business of deposit taking, and deposit taking is based on the payments system. Deposit money in banks gets its "use value"—the real reason we use it at all—from its role as the basis of payment, the ability to swap money for other stuff. All of the payments that we make and receive constitute, ultimately, the transfer of the right to some amount of deposit money from one person to another. How we actually make this transfer is less important than the fact that bank-deposit money is the "coin of the realm," the modern equivalent of gold, in the modern economy. This fact may or may not be a "good thing," but it is a fact nonetheless.

A Regulated Monopoly

All of this is why governments allow banks to have powers of monopoly and in turn regulates them more tightly than any other business. Bank privileges and regulation are both, at the bottom, meant to sustain a payment system that works and enjoys public confidence.

This goal leads to two things that really matter. First, only banks can take deposits from the public as a matter of law and regulation. The definition of *bank* may change from time to time and place to place, but this ability is the bottom line everywhere. If it is licensed by government to take deposits, it is a bank whatever else it does. Second, only banks have direct access to the books of the central bank. In the modern world, money is not tied to any source of value outside the deposit money system that is managed by central banks like the

Federal Reserve. Central bank money may be a fiction, resting on the faith and the credit that people place in their government, but that faith and credit, for better or worse, is as good as it gets. All full-fledged banks have deposit money accounts at the central bank of their country. This is the very core of the deposit money system, money on hand at the central bank. Central banks can increase the stock of deposit money simply by putting more money into these accounts held on its books. Central banks can make loans or buy market instruments from the banks. Banks in turn can multiply the deposit money they receive simply by making more loans to customers. Banks, in other words, are unique because only they can create money, deposit money, on their ledgers that other businesses and people can spend.

Money Creation

For example, if you take out a loan from a bank, what really happens is that the bank either creates deposit money in your account or it pays someone else in deposit money that the bank creates on your behalf, as with a home or auto loan. This is money that did not exist before. The money you owe the bank is essentially new money in the economy. If you borrowed the same money from a lender who wasn't a bank, they in turn would have to borrow that money from the money market or from a bank. They couldn't just create it by extending your credit.

Clearing and Settlement

Access to the books of the central bank also amounts to a monopoly position in the payment system. All payments in deposit money ultimately get settled up between banks through their accounts on the books of central banks. These accounts are the balance point upon which a giant mountain of payments rest. For example, during the month you may deposit a paycheck, get an insurance payment via the ACH, make a half dozen credit card payments, write ten checks, and use your ATM card for cash four times and four times at the store. Several thousand dollars in deposit money will flow through your accounts in the process, coming from or going to accounts at many different banks. However, the only real movements of deposit money between all these banks themselves will be a much smaller net amount on their accounts at the Federal Reserve.

All the checks into and out of accounts at banks go through a process called clearing and settlement, which means that banks exchange—"clear" in bank-speak—the checks they have on one another to determine which banks owe other banks any deposit money for that business day. This amount is usually a small fraction of the face value of the checks exchanged. The banks then "settle," bank-speak for those banks that owe others to pay up. This settlement is normally done using deposit money accounts held at the Federal Reserve. The ACH, which is really an electronic version of this check clearing house, also settles against Federal Reserve accounts. The ATM, debit, and credit card networks all do clearing settlement in a similar fashion. This way, a very small amount of deposit money at the Federal Reserve supports a vastly larger volume of payments in deposit money between banks and then with customers. The actual amount of money passed around is mind numbing.

WHY BANKS ARE SPECIAL

As we said previously, the United States produced about $13 trillion in goods and services in 2007. That is a very big number. However, it is dwarfed by the annual turnover in the payment system. In 2007, Americans paid each other $83 trillion in the "real economy." Because most daily payments we make are quite small and we make many of these small payments, over 340 billion transactions took place. All but about 100 billion of these payments used paper money and coins, but these "cash" transactions accounted for only one dollar in sixteen of turnover. The so-called non-cash payment system that runs on bank deposit money made up the rest, some $78 trillion, or six times the GDP. In other words, the U.S. real economy turns over a dollar of deposit money six times to produce a dollar of final output. This, not the availability of credit, is what makes governments worldwide move heaven and earth to keep their banks afloat. Banks are far from the only source of credit, and in fact most credit creation takes place outside the banks, but banks, and banks alone, create deposit money. If credit becomes hard to get, the economy slows down, as is now occurring. If the system of payment based on bank deposit money fell over, the whole economy would stop in its tracks.

What neither the average taxpayer nor the average politician seems able to grasp is that in reality, there is no such thing as money outside of deposits in the banking systems. In the modern world, there is no actual money. There are only promises to pay. These include $7.3 trillion the banks have promised to you and me in holding our deposits. Those promises are only credible—something we can have faith in—because they're made by banks that have the "faith and credit" of our society. Our money is the banks' money, and the banks' money is our money. We may dislike, even despise, banks and bankers. They do not warm our hearts. However, we are joined at the hip. No banks, no deposit money, no economy. No other industry is even remotely as important to us as banking.

How Banks Make Money

At the same time, vital as they are, banks feed richly on their deposit money monopoly. They get to eat the first and largest chunk of the household balance sheet that feeds the whole financial jungle. Deposit money is a very potent food for banks. A dollar of deposit money that is held by a customer to make her payments tomorrow can be used by a banker to make a loan or investment today. Banks, in other words, can make money using their customer's money. No other business can do this to quite the same degree. To Bagehot, the business of banking was a "privileged opportunity" to make money using the money of others. In fact, although banks are now involved in many more lines of business than in his day, they still make the lion's share of their revenue by holding and using other people's money—OPM for short. Banks in the United States, for example, make about half their revenue from holding, paying, and receiving deposit money for customers.

The Magic of OPM

The reason for this is simple: If I lend you a dollar of my own money, I have a dollar less to use for other things. The more I lend you, the less I have to spend until you can pay me back. So, if I am using my own money, lending you money is a lousy business unless I can charge sky-high rates and collect my loans. Unless I am the mob, this is not easy to pull off, so I may be better off just selling you things rather than lending you money with which to buy stuff from other people. However, if I can get other people to give me their money for safekeeping, then lending you their money is a very good business. When I lend OPM, I do not reduce the money I have for other purposes. My own money is only needed to convince other people that I am solid and can be trusted with their money. As Bagehot put it, a banker's money is there to *guarantee* the business, not to *work* the business. Capital, the relatively small amount of money that I really own, allows me to attract and to use a much, much larger sum of OPM if, and only if, I am a banker. In fact, the business of banking only begins when I am using OPM. Banks can be more or less defined as businesses that rent the use of OPM. A banking license is really a license to make good money without really have to do very much. Sure beats manufacturing and selling actual stuff.

However, like any "privileged opportunity," there are strings attached. One string is simply that banks need to make a profit. People prefer to put their money in a bank that isn't losing money. In fact, banks that lose big sums of money, especially when it is unexpected, can be quickly brought down by a "run on the bank." Depositors in these dramas rush to remove their money before the banks go bust, something that is *sure* to make it go bust. Bank runs brought down thousands of U.S. banks in the 1920s and 1930s, which is why the Federal Deposit Insurance Corporation (FDIC) was put in place to provide both oversight and deposit insurance to prevent them.

But it's not enough for banks to just avoid the rare disaster. Banks need to make enough money out of OPM to pay for the cost of running the payments system and other expenses. They also need to provide earnings growth and a dividend for the shareholders who give them capital. Since a bank can only make money out of OPM by renting the use of it to somebody, they need to find relatively safe ways to lend it out.

Renting Out Money

Banks rarely face a shortage of people who want to borrow money if they can get it. Finding people who will and can pay them back is

the real challenge. This means that banks need to walk a fine line between potential borrowers who represent a small enough risk of non-payment that all lenders will give them loans and those that really need credit but are so risky that they have a hard time finding lenders. The first will pay very little to rent the banks' OPM while the second will pay a lot. The bankers' problem is deciding how much risk of not being paid back is acceptable in return for a higher rent. This comes down to what banks call "credit underwriting." It is the hardest thing that a banker does to earn his living. Remember, the banker is not putting his own money at risk. He is lending OPM, which is to say, money that belongs to you and me. He owes us this deposit money and has to give it back to us whenever we want it. It would seem obvious that banks should limit themselves to risk-free loans and investments. Through most of banking history they did just that; making short-term loans to finance business transactions backed with valuable collateral. Over the last few decades, the banks discovered commercial lending couldn't make them enough money to cover their costs and grow their profits.

This is the Achilles heel of banking. Banks are not only tempted to make more risky kinds of loans to more risky borrowers; they are almost forced to do so by their shareholders. A bank management could, in theory, keep all their OPM in risk-free business loans to solid companies and government bonds. Fifty years ago that is what they all did. However, in today's world, or at least the world that existed before 2008, such a group of managers would be thrown out by the shareholders for making too little money on their investment. This pressure for high returns always pushes bankers "out the risk curve" in good times. This means that they gradually begin to lend more money to those who had previously been viewed as riskier customers and riskier propositions.

Banks do not do this consciously as much as they absorb the atmosphere of optimism from the general state of the economy in good times. What had seemed risky always feels less so in a booming economy. Banks also absorb a more confident attitude about risk from each other. Banks are herd animals. A feeling of safety for a banker comes from doing what all the other banks are doing. If one bank begins to make money doing something that banks had previously steered clear of in the way of lending, other banks are under great pressure to follow suit. It takes real courage to buck the herd. Even if the "new new thing" blows up, the bankers who simply did what everyone else was doing seldom lose their jobs.

This tendency to lend too easily when times are good is matched by an equally strong instinct for the bank herd to stampede away from lending markets when the economy turns down. In short, bank lending fuels an economic boom on the way up and fuels an economic bust when lending suddenly dries up. In the United States alone, banks have, over the last two generations, been burned on multiple occasions by commercial real estate booms, foreign lending booms, home mortgage lending booms, consumer credit booms, and other types of lending that earlier generations of bankers would never have touched. This was not out of corruption or stupidity. Bankers as a tribe are well educated and cautious people, and probably among the most ethical of business people and unquestionably among the most exposed to detailed regulatory oversight of their actions. In hindsight, many credit decisions taken in good times look risky later on, if not plain dumb.

Napoleon once said that a good soldier can do anything with a bayonet except sit on it. The same is doubly true of the OPM that sits on the books of banks. It costs banks real money to acquire OPM in the form of interest paid, providing payment services, and the huge regulatory overhead. Banks can't sit on it for long. They need to lend it out, at a profit. The next section will describe one reason why lending OPM at a safe but decent return has become such a challenge. We will describe the super predators of the financial jungle and how they came to dominance until their recent mass extinction.

THE INVESTMENT BANKS

When the average person hears the words Wall Street, he or she thinks of rich guys in suits gambling and scheming away their money. In fact, this is far off the mark. Wall Street is shorthand for a vast global market that brings together savings and ways to put those savings to work. This market is much larger than the banking system we just described. It does many of the same things and in some ways more efficiently. It pools together big chunks of borrowable money from millions of households and uses that money to finance businesses, consumers, and governments on a scale no bank could undertake. It transfers money from low-payback uses to high-payback uses. It provides ways to spread, balance, and manage big financial risks. It determines what companies, and financial instruments, and even currencies and commodities like gold and oil are worth at any given point in time. Increasingly, Wall Street has become global and able to move vast flows of money across national boundaries. Wall Street, for example, allowed tens of millions of prosperous American households to go on a home buying and credit card debt spree with the savings of hundreds of millions of poor Chinese.

Until the global market meltdown of 2008 effectively swept away the old Wall Street by turning investment banks into bank holding companies, the one great thing investment banks did *not* do is take deposits. Banks proper retained a monopoly on deposit money, so the denizens of Wall Street ultimately relied on banks for credit and payment services. This proved to be a critical weakness. However, until their overnight meltdown, the beasts who thrived in the Wall Street jungle took advantage of their lack of direct access to OPM. It allowed them to be more agile, far less regulated, and far more ruthless than banks. Of course, banks feed off the household balance sheet, but they arguably give you and me real stuff in return, such as the safety and convenience of deposit money payments. The beasts that ruled Wall Street were pure predators, red in tooth and claw. They devoured every available chunk of the household balance sheet, especially in the United States, and now most of them are gone. Such is the rise and fall of the American investment banking industry.

Investment banks, or in U.S. regulator-speak "broker dealers," are not, strictly speaking, banks at all. Until the panic period of 2008 (when they were allowed to become bank holding companies), investment banks could not, as we noted, take deposits. Real banks live off OPM. Investment banks live off financial markets. They do this in a variety of ways. First, they act as gate keepers to the financial markets, both national and global. Anyone needing a lot of money can find a bank to talk to about a loan. Banks are real places with an address and contact numbers. They might not give you money, but you can go to them directly without having to pay a gate keeper. The financial markets have no real physical existence beyond a few big buildings with floors of traders. These traders buy and sell something called "securities" or "financial instruments," the subject of the next chapter. These things are mostly bought and sold through computer screens and over the telephone, so the financial market is really nowhere and everywhere, just like a social network on the web. People with money looking to put it to work in the market and people looking for money to rent are brought together in a global web of electronic connections built to buy, sell, and store financial instruments such as stocks and bonds.

However, unlike a social network, people cannot just plug in directly and find someone to sell them money or buy their money (though there are websites that do just that for small loans). No, the financial markets are a rather exclusive club for high rollers. You cannot just walk in; you need to pay a gate keeper, a member of the club, to play for you. When I want to buy or sell a financial instrument, in almost all cases, I can only do so through a broker who is a member of a club that trades the instrument involved. We call these clubs exchanges. The most famous are stock exchanges like the New York Stock Exchange, but there are organized exchanges for trading everything from commodities to dry cargo rates. Most exchanges started their lives as clubs of brokers. Lately, many have morphed into for-profit businesses, but they are still largely run for the benefit of brokers.

Until a couple of decades ago, the broker side of being a "broker dealer" was pretty lucrative. People had to pay a broker a "commission" every time they bought or sold a "security." These commissions were mostly a fixed fee per unit bought and sold. Exchange-speak calls securities purchases and sales "trades." Normally, a broker with a "sell order" from one customer would find a broker with a "buy order" from a customer for the same security. They would agree to a price at which the seller would swap the security for the buyer's cash, based on the buyers "bid" and the sellers "offer." What makes an exchange of any kind work is that all this haggling or trading takes place within the same place, even if that place is an electronic screen, and with the same rules, with all the brokers able to see the most recent trades and the price at which they were done.

When the brokers had to be in the thick of a physical trading floor or "pit" to find prices for their customers, their fees or commissions made some sense. The problem is that modern information systems made it easy to bring buyers and sellers of securities together—to "match trades" in a computer system. As exchanges became electronic and efficient, the value of brokers to buyers and sellers fell, and so did the fees their customers were willing to pay. Fixed commissions have been abolished in most markets under pressure from regulators responding to investors. "Discount" brokers like Charles Schwab and E*trade increased competition on the retail side. The broker's life, once cushy, has been getting tougher for decades. Their response has been to increase the number of licensed brokers—so-called registered reps—selling securities to the public. The value of a broker to an investment bank is simply to make more trades happen and get clients to put more money into the firm. Brokers only survive by being "producers," meaning they get clients to trade as much as possible. This is probably not a good idea for most of us, but it is how brokers hang on to their jobs and get paid a bonus.

The Bonus Culture

Two points now need to be underlined. Most investment bank pay is bonus, just like many sales jobs. Think of David Mamet's *Glengarry, Glen Ross* or Danny DeVito in *Tin Men,* and you have the picture. Second, the investment banking model is by its very nature riddled with conflicts between what is good for the bank and what is good for the client. The customer always comes second.

Besides buying and selling securities for their customers, "broker dealers" have a second way of making money. They are wholesale "dealers" in the securities they buy and sell as "brokers." This, put simply, means two things. First, they "underwrite" and "issue" securities. "Underwriting" is the work of putting together a security that will allow a customer to attract money from investors. To "issue" is to put the security out in the market. Both of these things require something called "distribution," which comes down to having brokers to sell the stuff. They also require that the broker dealer "makes a market" by buying and selling the securities they underwrite and issue. They play as professional dealers in what is called the "secondary market," the market in which bankers and brokers buy and sell between themselves. This wholesale professional market dealing is the second basic way the broker dealers make money outside of broker fees.

The third traditional source of broker dealers' profits is so-called advisory work. This feeds upon and in turn feeds the business of bringing companies "to market." Broker dealer firms and pure advisory firms employ people whose job it is to win and retain the confidence of large corporations and governments by giving them advice about how to raise money, pay down debt, buy and sell companies, and restructure themselves in one way or another. These "rain makers" are supported by armies of number-crunchers, lawyers, and other specialists. They can only make their ideas and advice pay off by getting their clients to "do deals." When a deal happens, the advisory firm gets a fee based on the size of the transaction. These fees can be huge. No deals, no fees, no bonus, so the advisor is conflicted between looking out for the client and the need to make deals happen to produce revenue. His or her credibility and usefulness, however, depends on honest, objective advice. Because they are in the markets every day as brokers and dealers, the firms these advisors work in have visibility to something called "deal flow." They have a pulse on the market, on what things are worth today and likely to be worth tomorrow.

INSTITUTIONAL INVESTORS

As anyone who has been cold called over the phone by a stock broker knows, the whole world of investment banking we have just described is all about selling. Investment banks are always hustling: The brokers and dealers push trades, the advisory folks pitch ideas in the hope they will turn into deals. Everybody lives on a modest, fixed salary and makes their real income out of bonuses based on firm, team, and individual performance. The collective term for all this selling energy is, in Wall Street-speak, the "sell side" of the business. "Institutional investors" play on the other team, the "buy side." "Institutional investor" is just a fancy term for anyone other than a bank who pools OPM and gets paid to put it to work in the financial markets. Some of the "buy side" of the global financial markets resides inside of the banks themselves. Many banks "manage money" for wealthy clients and trusts. Broker dealers also have money-management businesses. However, the mother lode of "institutional" money on the buy side is that which millions of households put aside for retirement or a rainy day in pension funds, mutual funds, and insurance companies.

Together, these sums of money make the deposit money in the banking system proper seem modest.

YOUR PENSION FEEDS THE MARKET

At the end of 2007, U.S. households had about $6 trillion in the bank, mostly in various types of savings accounts. However, the actual reserves (that is, real money, not just promises) for pension funds was $13 trillion. Households also held $5 trillion in mutual funds and another $1.4 trillion in money market funds. Their life insurance policies held another $1.2 trillion in reserves. The "buy side" is huge, and for a very good reason. The only way anyone can continue to have an income after they stop working is to put aside money today that they can use later in life. If the average person needs $40,000 a year to live in retirement and will on average live twenty years, that means that they need $800,000 over that period. Obviously, you and I can't save that kind of cash. There are only two ways to solve the problem. One is pay-as-you-go "unfunded" government pensions like Social Security. These are classic Ponzi schemes, sort of Bernie Madoff on a much vaster scale. Today's payroll taxes are not invested; individuals have no accounts and don't have any legal right to a pension. Instead, people working today are taxed to pay benefits to people who are retired or on disability. As long as people mostly died before becoming eligible or didn't live long in retirement, this worked fine.

But the public doesn't understand this scheme for what it is. Politicians have for seventy years gotten away with talking about a "trust fund" with no real investment behind it, just treasury IOUs and "a lock box" that is always empty. Eventually, Congress will have to raise taxes through the roof on working families or stop paying anything like the current level of benefits. Most other countries have realized this already. So, pay-as-you-go schemes are in decline almost everywhere except the United States.

The second way to come up with $800,000 over twenty years is to accumulate a pile of real investments that will generate $40,000 per year. This will depend on two things: How much money is paid into the pile, by whom, and how much income it can generate.

The first issue is simple. If you have a company pension, your employer will put in some or all of the money. Of course, he can only do this by paying you less. If you do not have a company pension, which is most of us, you have to fund your own pension. The same applies if you work for yourself, of course. Congress has created a host of confusing tax-deferred schemes, some of which allow for a limited amount of "matching" by employers. Of course, you can always put all your extra money into the bank or into mutual funds. All these options do is determine how big the pile will get over time. Obviously, anything that your employer puts in and the ability to save without taxes helps a lot in making the pile grow.

The second issue, making the highest income per buck put into the pile, is critical. At a 4% return—higher than a bank would give you—you need $1,000,000 to generate $40,000 per year. At an 8% return—what the stock market has returned on average for the last century—only $500,000 is needed. If you can get a 16% return, something many money managers achieved in the last decade, you only need $250,000. In a nutshell, the whole game on the "buy side" is to maximize returns on the savings that are entrusted to them. The country—which is to say, you and me—simply doesn't save enough to retire on bank-type interest. All of us ultimately depend on the ability of institutional investors to earn high returns. Company pension plans, union pension plans, individual pension plans, insurance company annuities, and the whole not-for-profit sector like colleges and hospitals all rely on the ability of the "buy side" to maximize the amount of income generated by each dollar in the pile. Institutions that cannot match or beat the investment results of the overall market do not last long, and neither do the individual money managers working in them.

THE ENDLESS SEARCH FOR RETURNS

It is easy to say that "Wall Street" is greedy, and greed does indeed drive many individuals who work in finance. However, the real driver of the financial markets is the relentless demand for high returns on the buy side. And the buy side is, at bottom, you and me, the people hoping to retire some day. The "sell side" of the market may be greedier at heart, but the demand for high returns by the "buy side" is what drives the market. Decades ago, most pension plans and insurance companies limited themselves to nice, safe investments like government bonds and blue-chip (big-company, low-risk) stocks. Against a background of a quarter of a century of relatively low interest rates, institutional investors learned to take on bigger risks for higher returns.

THE SEARCH FOR YIELD

The upshot of its hunger for high returns is that the "buy side" got what it was looking for in the form of new products and new providers from the "sell side." In terms of products, the sell side learned to slice and dice loans (especially consumer loans like mortgages, car loans, student loans, and credit card debt) and turn them into high-yield but highly rated securities. This process, called "asset securitization," made the reckless expansion of consumer debt not only possible but almost irresistible because of buy-side demand. The investment banking wiz kids even invented whole new classes of securities called "derivatives." Derivatives have no value in themselves but allow investors to "bet" on the value of an asset or contract linked to them. For example, a credit default swap allows investors to make money if a company or country cannot pay its bond holders. The rapid fire invention and roll out of new, untested securities has been central both to the explosive growth of the global financial markets and the shocking meltdown we are now living through.

Hedge Funds

New providers—often called "alternative investment vehicles"—have also sprung up to meet the "buy-side" demand for higher returns on invested money. They are only open to professional or "sophisticated" investors, in part to escape regulation. The most notorious and widely reviled type of "alternative" investment provider is called a "hedge fund." The term itself originally meant a fund that could make bets or "hedges" in the markets that an ordinary, regulated mutual fund wasn't allowed to make. Today, it means a fund in which big-time investors expect to enjoy super-sized returns through the superior trading strategy of the fund manager. Often this strategy is essentially a "black box" based on complicated computer models the fund has uniquely developed. The investors are essentially acting on the belief that the manager has a "secret sauce" that allows him to beat the market. If he fully disclosed how it works, of course, the sauce wouldn't be a secret.

Too Many Cooks

A lot of sauce was being cooked up: There were only a handful of hedge funds with negligible assets in 1987 but by the end of 2007 they numbered 12,500 and held around $2.5 trillion. About half this money was invested through so-called funds of funds, hedge funds that invested in hedge funds! This seemed to suggest that a very large number of players in the casino were somehow beating the house since the value of the whole U.S. stock market was only 15 to 16 trillion dollars. For the hedge fund managers, the game was really a one-way bet. They were paid on a "2 plus 20" formula: The manager charged 2% on the money invested and got 20% of the gains his clients made. This meant a few thousand people were getting paid tens of billions a year to play the market with OPM. Successful managers routinely made hundreds of millions, in some cases billions, of dollars. Of course, they could lose money for their clients, but managers still got their fees and even had the right to restrict their clients from taking their own money out of funds. Amazing as it seems, in a low-interest-rate world full of investors hungry for high returns, hedge funds attracted the money of not just the greedy rich but also sober institutional investors like pension funds, college endowments, and even municipal governments.

Venture Capital

The second type of alternative investment fund did not invest in the markets like a hedge fund but instead put their money to work either funding new companies or buying old companies from their shareholders and making them more profitable. The business of funding new companies in their early days, or rather the business of turning ideas into businesses, is called venture capital. Its spiritual homes are Silicon Valley in California and Greater Boston in Massachusetts. It has given us EBay, Google, Amazon.com, and a host of biotechnology companies. It has also given us a host of financial dogs, including pets.com. At its best, venture capital fuels the creativity and dynamism of the U.S. economy. Its only contact with the capital markets is when the venture capitalist, a private investor risking his or her own money, want to "cash out" one of their companies by having the broker dealers "bring it to market." The dot.com boom and bust of the 1990s showed how this process gets out of hand, turning into a feeding frenzy for the investment bankers and a mania for the buy-side firms and individual investors. That said, a healthy venture capital industry was a real strength of the U.S. economy over the last quarter century.

Private Equity

Private equity firms are a more mixed blessing. At their best, they buy sound businesses that are under-performing and fix them so they can be sold at a higher price. At their worst, they buy control of companies that have weak stock prices, load them up with debt while stripping out assets, and flog the carcass off to someone else. The problem is that the good model of private equity takes real operating skills and a lot of patience. The bad model is all based on financial engineering, most notably juicing profits by operating the company on borrowed money. Institutional investors hungry for high returns were more likely to put money into the second model than the first, and banks hungry for lending opportunities were more than happy until quite recently to provide the OPM.

The common thread of all these alternative investments is that in a period of low interest rates and rising prices for financial assets, debt (or as the financial professionals say "leverage") was really their "secret sauce." Hedge funds and private equity firms both took advantage of cheap and plentiful bank credit to super-charge their returns. Remember, if I can operate a business on other people's money rather than my own, I make more returns on my capital. This simple rule got stretched to a ridiculous extent, largely well outside the view of regulators. The economy became, in a sense, one large hedge fund, leveraged to the hilt. Bank debt, which was only 21% of U.S. GDP in 1980, had exploded to 116% by 2007. Debt held outside the banking system accumulated even faster. Household debt rose from less than 60% of disposable income to a clearly unsustainable level of 133% over the same period.

The other thing that happened was that all the broker dealers and institutional investors, along with most of the largest commercial banks, became addicted to trading with each other in the financial casino as a means of increasing their profits. The dollar value of payment transactions processed by the world's bank-to-bank funds transfer systems consists almost entirely of settlement for financial trading by the largest global banks and investment banks. In 2003, over $774 trillion in dollar settlements were processed, but by 2007, an astounding $1,157 trillion turned over in the wholesale payments systems in New York. This is equivalent to turning over the entire U.S. economy about three times every business day of the year. New York Stock Exchange transaction volume leapt from $9.7 trillion to $29.9 trillion dollars over the same period.

Ultimately, this vast and accelerating global money pump rested on a relatively small and fragile base of bank deposit money and credit and an even smaller amount of "capital," real resources owned by the banks. As long as everyone had confidence in the markets and the future, all this trading and underlying leverage drove market prices for investment, and along with them incomes and jobs, to higher and higher levels. People had lost sight of the delicacy of the whole thing. The real question is not why the whole house of cards fell down in 2008, but why it stayed up for so long.

2

▼

THE FINANCIAL MARKET
MADE SIMPLE

FINANCIAL INSTRUMENTS

We have just seen how investment banks and institutional investors churn trillions of dollars through the global financial markets. They are not, of course, swapping piles of paper money. They are trading "financial instruments." If most of us do not understand what money is or how our bank account works, almost nobody has a clue about "financial instruments." The name itself is not helpful. "Financial" tells us it has to do with money, but what does "instrument" mean in this case? The word has many meanings, but broadly speaking, an instrument is the means by which something is done. A musical instrument is the means for making music; a legal instrument is a document that does something involving law, like a deed that gives you title to your house.

Contracts

The simplest way to think about financial instruments is that each basic type is a "contract in a box." All of us know what a contract is at some level. Marriage is a contract between two consenting partners, with rights and obligations that are supported, but not created by, law and social norms. Employment is another common contract; even if no formal employment contract is signed, the rights and obligations of employers and employees are pretty well understood by everyone and are governed by specific laws. That's what contracts do—lay out the deal. Almost any social arrangement you can think of, the U.S. Constitution to your kid's allowance, is an explicit or implicit contract. Contracts are the millions of deals that get done, making things happen. Although the vast majority of law and legal work revolves around contracts, the law usually only comes into play when one party to the deal feels the contract has been broken. Fortunately, most of the contracts we rely on each day happen pretty simply, so much so that we don't think of them as contracts at all. That is because they have become routine. If I work in a business, the deal is that I get paid. My boss expects me to work and expects to pay me. He expects to be paid by his customers, and is expected to pay his suppliers. All economic activity can be described in terms of a huge number of contracts—deals—being carried out routinely between people.

Contracts in a Box

However, just because we go through life routinely carrying out our side of deal does not make that deal or contract something we can trade or exchange with someone else. Most of our contracts in life are between two specific parties. We have specific spouses, bosses, and customers. This is why financial instruments have to be not just a contract, but a "contract in a box."

Liquidity

Financial instruments were not invented; they emerged through trial and error over the centuries. Some go back millennia. Those that have survived the test of time have one thing in common: They are "standard." They are "in a box," just like anything you buy off the shelf; the same stuff is always inside, they always work the same way. Being standard makes a financial instrument easy to buy and sell because lots of people understand what it is, how it works, and can put a price on it. Standard financial instruments—financial contracts in a box—are what is called "liquid" in finance-speak. This is a very squishy concept, but at bottom, all we mean by liquid is that something has lots of buyers and sellers. When you read in the paper or hear the TV news assert that the credit markets are "illiquid," this means that people who have money won't lend it to people who need it. There are no sellers and no buyers for a large variety of financial instruments. Thankfully, this is a pretty rare occurrence, and often means that the financial instruments themselves were flawed—a point we will return to in explaining the sources of the 2008 market crisis.

Standardization

The basic rule of financial contracting is that, over time, transactions—that is to say, the deals—become increasingly standardized. This is because the easier an instrument is to understand and the less specific the information needed to make a "deal or no deal" decision, the more they will attract buyers and sellers. In finance-speak, they will be liquid. When something is liquid, it means that, if you don't want to keep it, you can always find a buyer who will take it off your hands at some price. That is a big deal for a buyer of financial instruments because being stuck holding an instrument you don't want can be a very bad thing. This is in principle no different than why the stuff we buy in stores comes in boxes of a standard size and in a brand we know. It reduces the buyers risk if they know that what they are getting will always be the same. We see hundreds of different boxes when we go to the store, but normally, have a pretty good idea of what to expect when we make a purchase.

WHAT FINANCIAL INSTRUMENTS DO

Actually, financial instruments are a lot simpler to understand than the physical stuff we buy. We don't really know how our processed food is made (probably wouldn't eat it if we did), much less our DVD and iPod. There is really no excuse for not knowing how financial instruments are made and work because they are some of the simplest things we deal with in day-to-day life. The problem is that financial professionals don't want you to understand what they are doing, often because they don't have a clue themselves. All financial instruments perform one or more of four very basic things for the people using them:

1. Allow people to exchange one type of stuff for another with certainty and efficiency.

2. Allow people to transmit financial resources across time, far into the future, and across space.
3. Allow people to pool financial resources for big undertakings.
4. Allow people to manage and spread the financial risks in business and life.

No one type of financial instrument can help us do all of these things, but a remarkably few will allow us to accomplish all of them. Moreover, there is more than one way to accomplish many of these things, each with its own pros and cons. Most of the financial instruments we use today have been around in one form or another for centuries, some since ancient times. This stuff is not rocket science.

BILLS OF EXCHANGE

Just as all humans are believed to be descended from a common ancestor, the whole population of financial instruments is descended from one basic type of contract. Like our long lost ancestor, nobody seems to know what this instrument is. Ask the average American banker to tell you what a "bill of exchange" is and prepare to be greeted with a look of bovine incomprehension. Yet the bill of exchange is the mother of all financial instruments.

It works like this. When two businesses buy and sell from each other, especially when they are not in the same place, they need to solve two basic problems. First, they need to exchange goods for payment and payment for goods and, second, they need to bridge time and space. Cash doesn't solve these problems for most businesses. You and I can largely get by using cash in our daily lives, but we don't normally buy stuff to sell it to other people or to use as parts of things that we sell to other people. But almost all businesses do precisely that. They order parts and material today, pay rent and wages today, and hope to turn those outlays into sales and cash sometime in the future. Without an instrument that allowed businesses to get paid today for something that might take them months to turn into cash, very little business would actually get done, and few people would be employed. Indeed, a lack of credit is often what keeps poor countries poor; broad access to credit has helped drive the growth of our economy over the decades. The beauty of the bill of exchange is that, when it was widely used, it allowed businesses to pay each other using a financial instrument that provided both payment and credit, solving both our basic problems.

The First Paper Money

It was really a simple idea. A bill of exchange is a negotiable IOU between two businesses. Negotiable means that the person accepting the IOU can sell it, and the right to collect the money it promises to pay, to someone else, who can sell it to someone else, on down the line until the debt is actually due. The ability to sell—the technical term is to "discount" the IOU—is based on the fact that it is a credible promise to pay a specific sum of money on or after a specific date. This key concept is sometimes referred to as "sum certain date certain." A bill of exchange also states where and by whom the amount will be paid to whoever is the owner of it at the time it falls due. These basic features, plus the fact that the IOU was linked to a real business transaction involving real goods, made the bill of exchange credible. It was the first, and for centuries almost the only, widely used "paper money." The paper money that Marco Polo famously encountered in China, though, was very different, an outgrowth of state power, not commerce.

Bills of exchange were developed by practical businessmen long before there were banks. They were mostly used by merchants, especially those working in long-distance trade. For example, a merchant in medieval London night want to sell wool to a buyer in Italy who had a cloth-making business. It took a month to get wool by boat to Italy, a month to make it into gabardine cloth, and a month to sell it and get paid for it. The bill of exchange would, in this trade, be made out for ninety days under normal circumstances. Another London merchant might be buying wine from Bordeaux, France. It was in storage, ready to ship, and took little time to deliver and sell in England. Bills in that trade might only be 30 days long. Behind each bill there was real stuff, English wool, Italian cloth, French wine. Everyone knew what this stuff was worth since these were well-traded commodities, just like oil is today. This made these bills, in finance-speak, "self-liquidating" or "real bills" that were only intended to bridge time. It was always clear where the money to pay the bill would come from when it came due. This is turn made it easy for a merchant who was owed the money to sell it for cash instead of waiting 30, 60, or 90 days for it to become payable. At least this was the case if the business making out the IOU was trusted.

Enter the Banker

This is where bankers came in and how the bill of exchange bridged space as well as time. All reputations are essentially local. You know who you can trust in your own circle of neighbors and business associates. It is hard to make such judgments about people in other communities, much less other countries. Many early bankers started out as merchants who had intimate knowledge of the participants in specific trades. They knew which bills to discount and which they shouldn't touch. They knew all this because they had networks of trusted business partners and agents, often kinsmen, in key cities. This is how bills of exchange bridged space. The wool buyer in Milan would make his bill payable at the counters of a banker from Italy who had set up shop in London. In fact, so much of this went on back then that the banking district in London was called Lombard Street after the Italian province many bankers came from. The bank lending benchmark in Germany is still called the Lombard rate. Because they could get paid locally in English money, London merchants could carry on a huge trade with Italy without a lot of cash moving between countries.

The English also bought a lot of goods from Italy, including fine cloth. London merchants could pay for the stuff at the same banks, swapping claims on Italian merchants against Italian merchants' claims on them. Very little hard money, gold and silver, ever had to be moved between London and Milan, something that was both danger-ous and often illegal.

The Problem with Bills

So, if the bill of exchange was such a great solution, why is it virtu-ally extinct as a financial instrument? The answer to this is that it failed the "contract in a box" test. Once simpler "in a box" ways of solving the same basic problems emerged through trial and error, the bill of exchange lost ground.

The main reason that a bill of exchange is not a "contract in a box" is that every bill is based on a unique purchase and sale of goods between two unique parties. It is an IOU for a specific amount due for payment at a specific time and place. Although they were used by merchants around the known world for centuries as a kind of paper money to make payments and transfer money for others (for medieval knights, bills of exchange were how you got your Crusading cash out to the Middle East), this specificity had real drawbacks. Imagine trying to pay your mortgage using bills of exchange you had bought. One might be for too much, or payable after the mortgage due date. Others might be payable before the due date but not add up to the right amount. You would still have to make up the difference in hard cash.

What happened over time and in fits and starts is that the bill of exchange has been largely replaced by no less than four "contract in a box" solutions. Each of these do only a part of what the bill of exchange accomplished as a financial instrument. They have all created new problems to solve. However, and this is the decisive point, they were all highly standard, demanded limited special knowledge, and could be "mass produced."

Checks and Drafts

The first of these is the check, sometimes known as a "draft" when payable by a bank. We explained a bit about how your paycheck turns into deposit money in the last chapter. We don't usually think of it this way, but a check is an everyday example of a "financial instrument." It gives any person with legal possession of the check—the "holder in due course" in bank-speak—the right to be paid a specific sum of money from your bank account on or after the date on the check. It is very much like a bill of exchange precisely because it actually is a bill of exchange stripped down its bare essentials. Like a real bill, it is fully negotiable—the right or claim to your money represented by the check is easily bought and sold—and involves a sum, a certain date, and a certain payment at a specific bank. What makes it a "contract in a box" is that no specific commercial deal is involved. So, the amount of the check and the date payable are essentially arbitrary. So is the party to be paid. The ancient language of a bill of exchange such as "pay to the order of" are retained on a standard printed check, but the specifics of how much, to whom, and by when are left blank until you, the account holder, write them in. These blanks in the form vastly increase the flexibility of the check as a financial instrument for allowing people to make payments efficiently. You can write a check for any amount to pay anyone, anywhere, for any purpose without an underlying commercial exchange being involved. At the same time, the check lacks the bill of exchange's utility in bridging time, and it adds nothing to management of risk.

The Current Account

These other functions largely got absorbed into deposit banking and balance sheet lending. A checking account known as a current account almost everywhere outside the United States—is always framed by fine print called "terms and conditions," which most of us can't be bothered to read. This account agreement is a one-sided financial contract between you and the bank. The contract between you and your bank works like this: They will accept and hold your "deposits," that is, your financial claims on others, such as the paycheck we spoke of in the last chapter, or for that matter, a ten dollar bill, which is a claim on the government, in a ledger record or account. The sum recorded as a "credit balance" in this account is a legal claim you have on the bank or, in bank-speak, a "liability." A deposit, then, is a debt the bank owes you. The bank also undertakes to act on your valid instructions concerning your money. This means that the bank has a binding obligation to give the money back to you upon demand (as when you cash a check or go to the ATM) or to others you designate (your check or debit card swipe is an instruction to your bank to pay some of your money to others) or to transfer it to other accounts such as a savings account. For you, the account is safe and useful, being at the same time a store of value ("how much money do I have?") and a means of payment ("I'll write you a check"). As we saw in the last chapter, the bank gets to lend or invest any deposit money you leave with it without your specific knowledge or permission. That is why the contract is one sided: You agree to the terms setting out how you can operate your account, and you may even agree to pay certain fees, but the bank can do what it wants.

BANK INTERMEDIATION

Once you understand a financial contract between you and the bank this way, it is fairly easy to grasp the concept of "financial intermediation." In theory, you or anyone with surplus deposit money or cash at a given time could find somebody somewhere in the world who at the same moment needed to use that money more than you did and was willing to pay you for its use. In reality, most of us want to get on with our lives and have neither the time nor the knowledge to find people who will pay for us for the use of our extra money. Banks don't explicitly offer you a chance to make real money out of renting your surplus deposit money. They offer you the safety and convenience of a checking account instead. Then they use their superior information, connections, and focus to find somebody who is willing to pay for the use of your money and appears likely to pay it back. In the process, they become what are called in bank-speak "financial intermediaries." To people who have money, they offer deposit and payment services, and to people who need money, they offer loans. If they know what they are doing, they pay you the absolute minimum in interest, convenience, and service required to get you to hand your money over and then charge the people who need the money as much as they can get away with.

Overdraft Banking

In most banking systems, most of this "intermediation" mainly takes place within the "current account." Current in this case means the "running" balance of money flowing into and out of the account, like the current in a stream. Basically, a current account acts as a deposit when the customer has a positive balance—"in credit" in bank-speak—and acts as a loan when the customer has a negative balance—"in overdraft" in bank-speak. Overdraft lending on current accounts is an incredibly simple way to lend money compared with discounting bills of exchange, something that required experience and specific knowledge. Basically, the banker just decides to keep paying the customer's checks in overdraft up to a limit he or she is comfortable with given the customer's income and assets. Money flowing into the account reduces or eliminates the loan. Because it is so simple and thus easy to "mass produce" using standard rules of thumb, overdraft lending has gradually displaced discounting bills of exchange as a source of credit wherever deposit banking has taken root. Overdraft credit is the second "in a box" solution that absorbed a big slice of bill of exchange functionality, at least outside the United States.

The American Exception

Here in the United States, we developed an equivalent "in the box" solution in the form of promissory notes (many times, just private IOUs) in place of overdraft loans. This is basically because the National Bank Act of 1864 created, the first federal bank regulator, the Comptroller of the Currency to oversee federally chartered banks. Experience of hundreds of bank failures over the years taught successive comptrollers that American banks were too small and beholden to local interests and insiders on their boards to safely extend overdraft credit. They effectively banned overdraft banking in the late 1800s, making the United States almost the only country without current accounts.

While bank loans come in all sorts of variations, they are almost always made using promissory notes, a "contract in a box" financial instrument governed by a body of rules called the U.S. Uniform Commercial Code. Like bills of exchange, promissory notes are fully negotiable and allow loans to be bought and sold. Both overdraft lending and U.S. style bank loans take over the bill of exchange function of bridging time but add a lot of flexibility. Remember, bills of exchange tied to real transactions usually only gave the seller 30, 60, or 90 days credit and only for the value of actual sales. Lower sales automatically meant less credit, more sales more credit. Credit was joined at the hip to the real level of economic activity.

Term Loans

Overdrafts, while in theory day-to-day loans, could in practice be more or less open ended as long as the borrower could pledge collateral that covered the bank's risk of not being repaid. The link to commerce was weakened. Banks could, if they were not cautious, put too much credit into the economy based on an exaggerated notion of what assets used as collateral were really worth. Bank lending expanded beyond collateral as banks learned how to lend money to companies for a year or more based on something called "credit analysis" of their financial statement information. These "term loans" grew in both length and absolute size, not only bridging time but also allowing banks to effectively pool the surplus OPM of millions of savers to fund really big business undertakings like building new plants or developing real estate. Banks were able to build vast pools of OPM over and above that in checking or current accounts through inventing a variety of "contracts in a box" that basically offered higher rates of interest to people willing to let the bank keep their money for longer periods of time. This ultimately led to a totally new financial instrument, the certificate of deposit or CD. You probably don't think of your CD as a negotiable financial instrument, but it is, and it allows banks to literally buy deposits. And of course savings in the bank allows you to bridge time by accumulating money today that you can spend in the future. The pooling power of bank savings fueled the financing power of bank balance sheets far beyond anything bills of exchange could support.

THE PROBLEM OF BANK INTERMEDIATION

Classic bank balance sheet "intermediation" is really an interconnected web of financial "contracts in a box," each of which contracts does one thing—payment, lending, pooling, or bridging time—well enough for us to use, and want to use, banks. All these financial contracts are "bilateral," between either you the depositor or you the borrower and your bank. Your bank is always in the middle, standing between you and the market for money. That is why it is called an "intermediary" in bank-speak. This has some advantage for you, since the bank is ultimately on the hook to look after the safety of your deposits. It is a fiduciary in legal terms with a "duty of care" to protect your money. It also takes upon itself the task of managing and spreading the financial risk of investing your deposit money. There is value in these things, but they come at a steep price. Your contract with the bank is one sided and far from transparent. For example, as a depositor, you do not ask what percentage of your checking or savings account is invested in loans and what percentage in government securities. Nor do you ask what types of loans and securities these are, what risks they represent, and how much they are earning. That's just not the deal between you and your bank. On the other hand, as a borrower, you would never think to inquire into the bank's true cost of funds. Again, that's just not the deal.

Information Advantages

Banks take full advantage of the fact that your checking and savings accounts serve one purpose in your life and your loans quite another. In fact, you probably find yourself paying 10% or more on loans and credit card balances while at the same time receiving a couple of percentage points in interest on your checking and saving account balances with the same institution, without connecting the two. Most of us don't. The banks profit from this, but we let them do so through our lack of attention to our overall household financial position. To some degree, all bank profits stem from the massively one-sided information advantage they enjoy over you and me. Banks know how much money you have in your accounts down to the penny at any moment. They know how much money you owe, and what kind of risk you represent based on past financial behavior, income, and assets. They have spent billions as an industry on technology to warehouse and analyze data so they can learn even more about you. You know essentially nothing about them. To you a bank is a black box. Even if you try to read your bank's financial statements they will tell you nothing that is useful in judging the soundness of its business. The loans and investments on its balance sheet are a blind pool of risks that, as we have found to our detriment, even the bankers themselves don't understand.

Market Intermediation

Fortunately, bank balance sheet intermediation is only one of the two basic ways of accomplishing the four basic things that financial instruments allow us to do. The alternative to using bank balance sheet intermediation is using the financial markets. The financial markets allow people with money and people who need money to contract directly with each other using financial instruments and thus reduce or avoid one-sided financial contracts with a bank intermediary. Perhaps believing that the profits of balance sheet intermediation were ordained by God, bankers coined an especially ugly word—"disintermediation"—some thirty years ago to describe the process by which large and sophisticated corporate borrowers bypass them altogether to obtain funds from the public. In fact, over the last two generations or more, the story of finance in the United States and in the broader global economy has been one of the gradual but accelerating shift of financial contracting from banks to tradable financial instruments or contracts whose value (or lack thereof) is established in the market. This value "transparency" is the one great virtue of market intermediation over bank intermediation. However, for markets to work, financial instruments need to be simple and easy to price and trade. The less transparent they are as "contracts in a box," the more murky and dangerous market intermediation becomes. The inability of public markets and investors to understand and price complex and novel financial instruments helped turn an upturn in U.S. mortgage defaults during 2007 into a global financial crisis in 2008.

COMMERCIAL PAPER

The most basic market instrument is commercial paper or CP. Like the check, CP is the direct descendant of the bill of exchange but has all the key features of a "contract in a box." It is an IOU for a fixed period of time, usually anything from 30 to 180 days, that is sold by corporations to investors in the money market. In that, it is the same thing as a bill. However, it is a naked IOU, with no underlying transaction to pay it off. Instead of being "self-liquidating," CP is normally "rolled over," bank-speak for paying off one incident of borrowing with a new borrowing for the same amount. Investors buy commercial paper based on the fact that it is a short-term investment, which is always less risky, made mainly on its credit rating. In fact, credit-rating agencies in the United States largely started their lives by rating this kind of paper. Basically, only the largest and most well-capitalized banks and companies used to have "access" to the commercial paper market. Even these needed commitment from banks to lend them the money to pay off their paper to get top ratings.

Most of us have no idea what commercial paper is, but it was the most important financial instrument in bringing about our current financial crisis. It did so in two ways. First, it supercharged bank disintermediation. Big credit-worthy companies found it much cheaper and easier to obtain the money they needed directly from the market using CP than by borrowing from banks. This led banks to search for new ways to make money. Twenty-five years of searching had gotten the banks to the poor position they are today, many of them circling the drain.

Second, CP had been a building block in a Rube Goldberg scheme called "asset securitization," another ugly phrase, this time relating to complicated financial machinery that transforms bank loans into marketable "financial instruments." Asset securitization is what allowed the great credit bubble of recent decades to inflate and then collapse, with asset securitization causing the bubble to pop and tank the real economy in the process. Commercial paper was an essential ingredient in the whole witches brew, as we will see later. Who bought all these naked IOUs? The short answer is that you did. Money market funds, which so many of us used to get higher returns on our savings, were among the biggest buyers of CP. The riskier the CP issuer, the higher the rate they paid us. Nobody questioned this when times were good.

BONDS

If you watch the TV money shows, you will see how much drama surrounds the trading floor the New York Stock Exchange. People clap when the bell goes off at 9:30. People run around. Prices of stocks and the major price indexes flash on the screen. Pundits prattle. The stock market is a dramatic place, even in a depression. However, long before there were "corporate equities," to use the finance-speak for stocks, there was a public market in the financial instruments that we call bonds. Bonds are the bedrock "financial instrument" in any economy, the ultimate "contract in a box." The basic concept of a bond is very simple, but it is rarely explained. The jargon used by the bond market and investment bankers doesn't help us understand them either. Bonds are just another financial contract. The seller of a bond is trying to get their hands on a large amount of money all at once. The earliest bonds were sold by governments to finance wars, which are by nature fairly short but very expensive. The buyer of a bond has a need for future income and is willing to put up money for it today. So the bond buyer is really buying a series of fixed interest payments that might continue for many years, and even in a few cases forever. That is why investment bankers call the bond business "fixed income." The rate of interest is often referred to as the "coupon," referring to the time when bonds were printed with paper coupons that had to be cut out and presented to the bond issuers when each interest payment fell due. That is why the idle rich are still sometimes referred to as "coupon clippers."

Bonds and Risk

Unless the bond issuer stops paying the coupon—in finance-speak, the issuer "defaults"—bonds are a dull, steady source of income. The probability of default (and the potential for loss of income and principal in the event of default) is what determines a bond's rating. The market for bonds worldwide assumes that a few countries worldwide, led by the United States, have effectively no risk of default. The rate of interest that "risk-free" borrowers have to pay to attract money is therefore limited to other factors. These are the threat of the government piling on too much debt and of the government "printing" too much money. Both of these are likely to drive down the real value of the interest received from the bond. In the first case, more borrowing is likely to drive up the rates the government needs to pay to suck in money, reducing the value of the coupon the bondholder is getting compared with what he could get tomorrow. The second creates inflation—too many dollars chasing too little stuff—which erodes the real value of the income received from the coupon. At some point, as happened in the United States during the 1970s, investors will stop buying "risk-free" government bonds. Bond investors hate to fund runaway government spending. This makes those so-called bond vigilantes, who keep a hawk's eye on government spending and loose money, very powerful. Governments that can't borrow except at crushing interest rates are in real trouble.

Bond Yields

If it is working well, the bond market sets all other interest rates. This means that for any "tenor"—the length of time the government wants the money—what it is required to pay is a benchmark against which all other interest rates are pegged. In the United States, the thirty-year bond is the longest dated government bond—often called the long bond. Other tenors for government bonds should pay less interest to bond buyers, all things being equal. All other borrowers going to the bond market should, for any given tenor, have to pay bond buyers more for their money than the risk-free government rate. How much more depends on their specific credit rating but most critically on current market sentiment about risk in general. The effective rate that the government has to pay to borrow money for any given tenor can be plotted as a line called the "yield curve." Normally, the curve should run from left to right, with rates going up with tenor. However, at times, we can have what is called an "inverted" yield curve, where shorter rates are higher than longer rates. This is because bond rates are set by the market, which is to say by you and me. Although you can buy government debt directly from the treasury, very few people do so. However, all institutional investors, from pension funds to banks and insurance companies are big buyers of government bonds. It's the only safe place to park money that you can't afford to lose. Therefore, at least some portion of your pension savings, insurance premiums, and bank deposits are put into the government bond market at any given time. The actual "yield" on government bonds is dictated by these buyers.

Bond Prices

The government mainly sells its bonds to the market through auctions in which a group of banks and investment banks bid for a share of the issue, the amount of bonds the government is trying to sell. These so-called primary dealers then sell bonds they don't want to hold in a "secondary market." The coupon that the government needs to pay to successfully auction off the issue is really a matter of informed guesswork on the part of the U.S. Treasury and the New York Federal Reserve Bank, which conducts the actual auctions. The real yield on a bond depends critically on investor demand. This in turn depends on market sentiment or confidence.

When investors are betting that inflation and government borrowing will get out of control, they will not bid on bonds that do not have high coupons to compensate them for this risk. The price they will pay at auction and in the secondary market for an issue may fall below the face value of the bonds. For example, $1,000 in 10% thirty-year bonds might only be worth $950 in the market. That makes the "effective yield" on the bond—the value of the payment stream I am buying—not $100 but $100 plus $50 as spread over the life of the bond. In contrast, if investors find themselves in a market panic situation, they will all want to buy government bonds as one of the few safe places to park their money. This "flight to quality" can easily result in government bonds being bid well above their face value with very low coupons, so they in effect pay investors nothing.

Of course, earning nothing is a good deal if everything else is falling like a stone. Unless a borrower simply refuses to pay their bondholders, as the Soviet Union did after the Russian Revolution, bonds are always worth something. Even if a so-called sovereign default does take place, most countries eventually pay their bond holders some portion of what they are owed. In contrast, corporations that issue bonds can and do default all the time, especially on the high-yield, high-risk end of the market known as "junk" bonds. However, even in a bankruptcy, bondholders are in line to get paid from the failed company's assets. Investors rarely lose their principal investment in highly rated bonds, in fact, if they hold them to maturity. If you put $1,000 into a highly rated bond that matures in twenty years, you will most likely get your $1,000 back in 2029. But the bond could still be a lousy investment if your money could have grown more over 20 years if it were invested in something else.

Bond Trading

That is why the real profits in the bond markets (and the real losses) come from trading bonds. Bonds of all sorts, mostly issued by governments and their agencies, are by far the biggest pool of financial instruments in most national financial markets and in the world as a whole. In finance-speak, bonds are by far the biggest "asset class." They are the epitome of a "contract in a box" because they are a simple, fixed-interest contract of debt. Only the name of the issuer, their rating, the tenor, the currency, and the coupon need to be specified for any bond issued in any country to find a market price. They are easy to trade precisely because the players in the bond market need so little specific information.

The motive behind all the trading in the bond market is simple. All of the institutional investors we mentioned in the last chapter are under pressure to squeeze as much yield as possible out of the OPM they preside over. By making informed bets on the direction of interest rates and inflation, smart traders can—if they get it right—keep their bond portfolio balanced to deliver higher returns. They can also enter into other trades to "hedge" their bond portfolios. Institutional investors make substantial amounts of their profits (and their losses) by trading bonds. Investment banks have huge bond-trading operations both to serve these buy-side players and to make money in so-called proprietary trading, essentially by making market bets with their own capital. Because the market is vast and relatively simple, traders have to churn through vast amounts of standard debt instruments to make their bets worthwhile under normal conditions.

The big money made by the investment banks over the last decade or so in large part came from inventing new, preferably mind-numbingly complex, financial instruments that were hard to price and trade but offered high returns A great deal of the severity of the 2008 meltdown was rooted in investment banks' remarkable inventiveness in creating and flogging new classes of bonds that had never before existed.

STOCKS

Stocks, or, in finance-speak, "corporate equities," are probably the financial instrument that many of us think we understand well enough to buy and sell on our own. There is a vast retail investment industry in this instrument, including stock brokers, financial advisors, and mutual fund companies, all dedicated to getting you to put your money in stocks. During the twenty-five-year global stock market boom that ended in 2008, this industry did very, very well. Until the recent and ongoing market meltdown, most of their customers also did well, but how many of these retail investors really knew what they are getting themselves into through buying stocks is another question.

At first glace, a share certificate, a simple title to ownership of a fraction of a company, is a simple "contract in a box." When you buy a share of stock, you are buying in reality two things. First, your share represents ownership in a business enterprise, including a vote in how it is managed. If the enterprise increases in value over time for any reason, you get to share in that increase. That is why business enterprises ought to be and mostly are managed to maximize shareholder value. The conventional measure of the shareholder value created or destroyed by an enterprise is called market capitalization or market cap. This is simply the market price of a share multiplied by all the shares of the company in the market, in finance-speak "outstanding." However, you are also buying a claim on the current and future earnings of the enterprise.

Stock Prices

In principle, the price of a stock should reflect the market view of a company's ability to grow its earnings. But even if a company fails to grow its earnings, it may still earn enough to provide a steady income stream to shareholders in the form of dividends. These are cash distributions to shareholders of company profits. The goals of growing the long-term value of the enterprise and that of providing the investors with a share of the profits can and do conflict with each other. If you think that a company that is growing rapidly in market value can sustain or accelerate that growth by reinvesting all its profits in the business, you don't want it to pay you a dividend. High-tech "growth companies" like Microsoft never paid dividends for precisely that reason: Their shareholders were buying future growth. Large, profitable companies in slow-growth industries are more or less obliged to return a large share of their earnings to their shareholders in the form of dividends. People own the shares mainly for income, just as they would a bond.

Why Stocks Are Risky

Unlike a bond, which is a contract of debt giving the bond buyer defined rights to be paid the principal and interest specified in the instrument, stocks are a pure ownership interest in an enterprise that may be worth a great deal tomorrow or nothing at all. There are never any guarantees that stocks will retain any value for their owners. If a company fails, and over time most companies either fail or are taken over, its shareholders stand to lose their entire investment. In a prolonged slump, even the best companies can fail. That is why stocks are always the riskiest financial instruments by their very nature. If a company fails, the common shareholders are absolutely last in line to be paid out of the assets of the firm. This risk, in theory, is more than offset by the chance that buying into a stock at the right time will make you a killing, especially if you can "get in on the ground floor" when a new company is "brought to market" in what is called an initial public offering or IPO. In reality, company insiders almost always capture the lion's share of any new stock issue. However, great fortunes have been amassed by canny investors like Warren Buffett in the equity markets of the world. Such investors are a kind of celebrity in some circles. Both the upside and the downside of equity investing are pretty much unbounded. Stocks offer real excitement and feed our dreams of riches. They are a bet on the future. Bonds by contrast offer "fixed income."

Stocks versus Bonds

That contrast is why, in the short run, the prices for stocks and bonds tend to move in opposite directions. Markets are always in flux between fear and greed. When people are optimistic about the future prospects of the economy, fear takes a back seat. Stock markets become convinced that the prices of almost all shares can only go higher. In such bull markets—and we are just coming off the longest bull market for corporate equities in history, going all the way back to Ronald Reagan's first term, with only a few brief interruptions—everyone believes that they can always make more money in stocks than in bonds. As a result, the demand for bonds and their prices is depressed. This can actually be good for yields. Bear markets in stocks, especially sudden panics, send investors stampeding out of equities and into bonds, especially risk-free government bonds, bidding up bond prices and driving down yields. Most of us, all things being equal, are buying financial instruments with money we have today so that we will have the money we need tomorrow, and the more money the better. Sooner or later, low stock prices will tempt money out of low-yielding bonds and bank deposits.

VOLATILITY

Because of this, prices for the two basic types of market-based financial instruments tend to be in a rough balance or equilibrium over long periods of time. If you need a certain amount of money to retire in 20 years, your money has to grow at a certain rate between now and then, which you can figure out without too much trouble (there is lots of software out there to help). You don't really care whether stocks, bonds, or for that matter bank CDs get you there as long as you accumulate enough to meet your goal. However, these financial instruments all represent very different levels of perceived risk and return, from low risk, low return to high risk, high return. Remember, nobody can predict the future, so the risk perceptions of everybody in the market—emotional factors, really—drive the tradeoffs that people make. These swings in sentiment create a lot of swings and round-abouts in the price of financial instruments, what market pro-fessionals call "volatility." Volatility has reached astounding levels, especially in world stock markets, since the summer of 2007.

However, over longer time periods, short-term volatility is mostly noise, and equilibrium actually rules. It works like this. If a company issuing stock is earning good money today and seems on track to keep doing so, its stock price should factor in those earnings. Remember, the stock is essentially an ownership stake in future earnings of the firm. The key measure is called the "price earning ratio" or "P/E" of a stock. High P/Es mean the market thinks the stock will make a lot of money in the future, so people are willing to pay a lot for it. Low P/Es mean the market is, for one reason or another, unwilling to pay much for future earnings. Individual stocks and indeed the whole market are said to be "expensive" or "cheap" based on how current P/Es measure up to expected earnings and historical norms. Where equi-librium enters the picture is the point at which stock prices are getting so far ahead of real corporate earnings that you are paying more and more in real money today for every dollar of future earnings, which begins to look questionable. At some point, you are paying so much that you would actually get more bang for your buck by putting your money into the bond market, reducing your risks in the bargain. If you have to pay $100 dollars today for $5 in current earnings, a P/E of 20 to 1 in simple terms, a 6% per year bond looks inviting. Put another way, over the long haul, there is a single, more or less natural market price investors can use for buying or renting the use of our money according to what the economists call the "efficient market" theory.

THE TEMPTATION OF RICHES

In reality, of course, you and I don't think this way at all. We don't just want to accumulate the wealth we need for a decent retirement. We want to get rich, if we can. Stocks always offer the hope we can do so by being clever or lucky. Stocks offer glamour and excitement. Without the drama of the Dow Jones Industrials and other indexes of stock prices bouncing up and down on the TV screen, how many of us would tune in to listen to Becky Quick? Stock investing is not as rational as the efficient market theory would suggest. It is a cross between a competitive sport and a lottery. Like other forms of gaming, it can be addictive.

PLAYING THE MARKET

There are at least four basic ways to play the stock market game, with many variants in between. The first, "momentum investing," is an attempt to win the game by simply buying what is going up. You don't really care if the firm issuing the stock has real, much less sustainable, earnings. This was the technology stock game of the so-called dot.com bubble. Momentum investors don't really worry about bubbles because either they count on less savvy investors to buy their shares before the bottom falls out, or they really believe that stocks are only going to go up.

The opposite of momentum investing is a second approach to the game, so-called value investing. This assumes that the markets are irrational and inefficient enough that in-depth analysis of a company's financial statements and market factors will allow you to ferret out stocks that are significantly "undervalued" by the market and buy them cheaply before the market catches up with reality. Most professionals who manage money for institutional investors and mutual funds play some variation of this game. Picking good stocks is what they are paid handsomely to do. Their key assumption in this approach is that, with hard work and smarts, you can beat the market.

Many market veterans and observers believe this simply can't be done consistently. Some of them rely on a third game plan, which involves something called "technical analysis." Its practitioners are sometimes called "chartists" because of the way they display their findings in "charts." Chartists assume that that equity markets move in patterns that can be observed and projected from historical price data. Both individual stock prices and the overall market is working relative to benchmarks like historical P/E ratios and their total returns relative to the returns of bonds. Analysis of these patterns can be very big brain stuff. However, most observers believe that it is pretty much impossible to predict in advance when to get into or out of the market, let alone a single stock.

The fourth basic style of play is called "index investing," essentially, buying a big basket of stocks that mirror the whole market. There are fund managers that do this for you. Or you can purchase shares in a so-called ETF, or exchange traded fund, that can be bought and sold like ordinary stocks but represent a claim on a basket of stocks.

CONVENTIONAL WISDOM

However you play the stock market game, the professionals tell us that certain things are always a good idea. For example, you are supposed to "diversify" your risks by owning a wide spread of stocks in different types of industries such as "financials," "technology" and "healthcare" with different characteristics. For example, big companies are called "large cap" because their total "market cap" (shares outstanding multiplied by the price) is very sizable. These companies normally differ in performance from so-called small-cap or mid-cap stocks. Stocks are also characterized as "growth" or "value" investments. Several labels can and do apply at once, so you can, for example, have a large-cap growth stock in tech. Investment advisors make their living off this stuff, as does the mutual fund industry, since owning mutual fund shares is one of the few ways you or I can diversify our portfolio with a relatively modest nest egg. In fact, the mutual fund industry has managed to produce more funds—all of which are essentially investment cocktails mixed up according to one or more of the game plans outlined above—than there are individual stocks. If you are an investor in such funds, you pay handsomely for their "secret sauce." The problem is that really rich people often get that way by having all their eggs in one basket (think of Bill Gates) or a few big holdings in which they have some clout over management (think Warren Buffett). So diversification may actually reduce your upside. In a real, full-bore market panic like the Fall of 2008, almost all stocks and classes of stock tank, so diversification offers little if any shelter.

IRRATIONAL MARKETS

Sometimes it's better to be lucky than to be good. The stock market is not rational. You have probably seen data and charts produced by financial advisors showing that equities have outperformed bonds by a significant margin over the last century or more. From this, you might conclude they represent a fundamentally better "asset class" for growing your money. What you are not told is that over that period most of the total growth in the value of stock market took place on a handful of days. Most of the losses took place in a few days during sudden panics and sell-offs. The averages over a century tell you almost nothing. If you missed the upswings and were caught in a big downdraft, you would have done better in fixed income. The point is that all financial instruments involve risk/reward tradeoffs. There are no safe bets that have big upsides.

Because the risk/reward tradeoffs of stocks and bonds are never ideal for either issuers or investors, the markets have over the years developed "hybrid" classes of financial instruments that are neither debt nor equity instruments. These are mainly used to tap the money of big institutional investors. Preferred stock, for example, gives investors a type of equity in a company that has none of the voting rights of "common" or ordinary stock but guarantees a higher dividend and and lets investors stand just behind the bondholders in case of liquidation of the business. Preferred stock is often convertible into common stock. Bonds have their own hybrids, such as convertible bonds that can be turned into stock under certain conditions. You can't buy these things, but institutional investors like your life insurance company can and do in the effort to better manage risk and return. The point is that the two basic "contracts in a box" financial instruments, stocks and bonds, can be used as basic building blocks in a variety of customized financial instruments and contracts. The more customized they are, the less tradable they become in public markets.

The two basic "contracts in a box," stocks and bonds, are traded in huge volumes every day in the public markets. That's one of the things that make them useful to you and me. We, or the people who manage our money, can always put a price on them because millions of buyers and sellers set that price in the market. Market traders are not like you and me, or for that matter like most institutional investors. Most of us put together a bunch of investments—"portfolio" is the fancy word—that we hope will over time produce the money we need tomorrow. We may trade in and out of specific financial instruments in the hope of a better portfolio risk/reward balance, but few of us like the market to be too exciting. Ups and downs make us nervous. Market traders live for the ups and downs. In a word, they are "speculators."

THE USES OF SPECULATION

Some people, politicians prominently among them, use "speculator" as a bad word applied to evil men cheating honest folk. Actually, speculation has a respectable Latin root, speculari, which means "to see." Speculation is the art of making money by seeing things in the future. For example, as we saw above, the price of government debt rests on a view of the future that is shared more or less by most market participants. Everyone knows that if the government suddenly jacks up spending and has to borrow, it will bid up interest rates. This will make bonds with lower rates less valuable. If I guess that this will happen tomorrow, I will sell these bonds today. The price I can sell at depends on how many bond buyers agree with my bet about the future and how many take the opposite view. Without such bets on the future being made all the time by market speculators, prices wouldn't move enough or often enough to keep Ms. Quick on TV. More to the point, speculators allow the rest of us to hedge our bets. Hedging your bets as an investor means buying a contract that offsets or otherwise limits the damage if the market in a financial instrument goes against you. You can only do this if somebody is willing to "take the other side of the trade," and in many cases that somebody will be a market trader or "speculator." In other words, a speculator's bet allows you to reduce your risk. No market can operate without speculators.

TOOLS OF THE TRADE: OPTIONS AND FUTURES

The basic tools of market hedging are financial contracts called "options" and "futures." Both have been around since the 1600s or earlier. An option is a contract that confers the right to buy or sell something in the future at a price you agree to today. For example, if you own a stock that you fear might be worth less in a year, you can hedge this risk by purchasing the right to sell it to me a year from now at today's price. I will sell you this right if I believe that the stock is cheaper now than it will be then. This contract is called a "put option" because you can "put" the stock to me to take at that price. The opposite type of contract is a "call option" in which you purchase the right to buy a stock from me at a certain price. There are many flavors of options, but essentially they are not financial instruments but side bets on the value of financial instruments. Most options can be traded independently of the real financial instruments they relate to, and few are actually "exercised," finance-speak for actually buying and selling under the terms of the option contract. Instead, they are mostly allowed to "expire" unexercised.

"Futures" are a variation on the theme of buying and selling something without really ever owning it. Futures markets started centuries ago in agriculture when grain merchants and other traders bought farmers' crops and livestock when they were still in the ground and on the hoof to lock in prices. Farmers used these futures contracts both to lock in their future incomes and to raise cash. Organized commodity exchanges like the Chicago Mercantile Exchange invented standard commodity futures contracts that could be traded like stocks and bonds, yet another example of the "contract in a box" principle in action. Over time, the number of commodity contracts that could be traded expanded to include stuff like metals, frozen orange juice, oil, and natural gas. Very few futures contracts ever result in delivery. If they did, Chicago, the world capital of commodity trading, would be buried in grain and live cattle, and hogs would fill the Loop. Instead, commodity futures markets make the much smaller "cash markets" more liquid by setting prices and allowing buyers and sellers to hedge their bets. It can do so because the world market for futures is and always has been a Mecca for speculators.

DERIVATIVES

You have probably been told by the clueless media that an evil financial voodoo called "derivatives" had a lot to do with our current financial crisis. This is largely nonsense. The futures contracts that we have just described are derivatives and have been usefully employed for centuries by buyers and sellers of all sorts of commodities and financial instruments to make markets work better. A "derivative" is simply a contract that "derives" its value from an underlying asset. Cattle futures ultimately get their value from the price of real beef cattle. Over the last thirty years and especially over the last decade, more and more futures contracts have been invented to allow financial market participants to make and hedge bets on the value of financial instruments, including stocks and bonds as well as entire stock and bond "baskets" and indexes. Foreign exchange and interest rates can also be hedged in futures markets. Derivatives have also been designed to allow companies to buy and sell "protection" against credit default by large public market borrowers including counties, banks, and corporations.

Thus far, these sorts of derivatives, although written in staggering absolute numbers, have not yet caused serious problems for the financial system. For the most part, they are pretty basic "contracts in a box" with reasonably standard terms and documentation. In fact, options, futures, and other derivatives are the only market financial contracts that help people to manage their financial risks, the fourth basic thing that financial instruments do for us.

Where the world of derivatives went bad was in writing contracts to hedge the risks involved in novel, overly complex, and untested financial instruments that were invented essentially to turn individually risky consumer loans into highly rated bonds.

MORTGAGES

The so-called sub-prime mortgage market deterioration that set in after U.S. house prices stopped rising in 2006 is often cited as the trigger event of the 2008 global financial crisis. How can a home loan be so dangerous? No financial instrument is less exotic. The mortgage is one of the oldest, most familiar, but least understood of financial contracts. Mortgages have been around since the Middle Ages. The word means "dead pledge" in Old French. Historically, mortgages had nothing to do with buying real estate. Mortgages were for many centuries a way for landowners to borrow cash against property they already had.

Today, you have a mortgage because it allows you to purchase a house, the cost of which vastly exceeds your annual income. At the same time, mortgage lenders will put up the money for your purchase because you pledge the house to them as security for a long-term loan. The lender can take the house if you fail to pay the interest and principal. You are signing up for a large and regular financial outflow for up to thirty years that cumulatively will be far greater than the current value of the house. From your point of view, however, the contract makes sense because you cannot otherwise buy the house and have use of it. The lender gets a steady cash payment stream over a long period of time, backed by security in the form of the house.

Mortgages for Everyone

How then did most of us come to have a mortgage? Widespread use of mortgages for house purchase only goes back to late nineteenth-century Britain. There, mutual savings associations called "building societies" began pooling the savings of ordinary working families to provide mortgages for houses they could afford, a classic example of the third basic function of financial instruments. The idea spread to the United States, and the savings and loan (often called S&L), or "thrift industry," was born. George Bailey's "Building and Loan" in the movie *It's a Wonderful Life* is an idealized example of these mostly small institutions. The plot of the movie also illustrates their Achilles' heel. A mortgage is a very long-term financial contract, but consumer savings can be withdrawn with little or no notice. Lending long and borrowing short is about the riskiest thing you can do as a bank. During the Great Depression, mortgage defaults brought down many lenders, and mortgage lending almost dried up. The New Deal established Federal Home Loan Banks to advance lenders money against existing mortgages to make more home loans available. This government involvement in promoting housing loans was popular and expanded after World War II with programs for veterans.

ENTER CONGRESS

During the late 1960s and 1970s, massive inflation again caused huge funding problems for the S&L industry. Congress responded by chartering two so-called government sponsored enterprises or GSEs (private sector companies with implied government guarantees) called Fannie Mae and Freddie Mac in 1968 and 1970 to guarantee and refinance mortgages generated by the thrift industry. Their stated aim was to make home loans more affordable without actually using the federal budget to do so. The GSEs may or may not have actually made house loans cheaper, but they did do two things. First and most critically, they developed standard terms and conditions for mortgages they bought or guaranteed. This allowed "contracts in a box" to be developed around these loans. Second, with government backing, the GSEs developed a "secondary market" for mortgages (remember, the secondary market allows initial lenders to find somebody else to take a contract off their hands, vastly reducing their risks).

MORTGAGE-BACKED SECURITIES

In the early 1980s, Wall Street pioneer Lewis Raniere at Salomon Brothers went a step further and transformed what had been a loan secured by real estate into a tradable financial instrument, in fact, a bond. The new animal was called a mortgage-backed security or MBS, a security representing a large pool of standard mortgages. Interest and principal payments from these mortgages created cash flows, which provided monthly payments to the bondholders. Thus, through a series of historical accidents, the mortgage became feedstock for just another investment security traded in the market rather than a unique contract between a lender and a borrower.

In fact, the mortgage-backed security established the template for a more generalized process of asset securitization thas has come to be applied to all kinds of bank loans, ranging from car loans and credit card receivables to wholesale trade receivables of corporations. As soon as both banks and Wall Street realized that the securitization "financial sausage machine" could be tweaked to manufacture marketable debt securities out of almost any type of loan, a wholesale migration of credit from bank balance sheets into the financial markets was set off. In the late twentieth century, the big brains in finance all thought that financial market intermediation had permanently gained the upper hand on bank balance sheet intermediation through the "financial innovation" that started with mortgages. They were wrong. It turns out that the asset securitization model provided the explosives to blow up the global economy.

3

▼

FINANCIAL INNOVATION
MADE EASY

"The business of banking ought to be simple; if it is *hard* it is *wrong*. The only securities which a banker, using money that he may be asked at short notice to repay, ought to touch, are those which are easily saleable and easily intelligible."

—Walter Bagehot, *The Economist*, January 9, 1869.

In the last chapter, we saw that so-called financial instruments were, at one time, in fact standard "contracts in a box" that were easily saleable *because* they were easily intelligible. In other words, there was no doubt about how to put a price on them, how they worked, and what risks were involved. In fact, financial contracts that could be standardized were always standardized. That is the straight line of financial evolution.

BANKING GETS HARD

Then suddenly, around 1980, hundreds of years of evolution were thrown into reverse. Clever bankers and investment bankers began to make things *hard*. They broke open all the "contracts in a box" that had stood the tests of time and began tinkering with them.

59

For example, bank loans used to be simple and easy to understand. They only came in a few flavors, like secured and unsecured. Suddenly, concepts like "structured finance" and "financial engineering" began to seep into the banker's vocabulary. So did the notion that banks could do things called "product innovation," "manufacturing," "distribution" and "channel management." These concepts had no roots in the traditions of banking and finance. In fact, many of them were imported into banking from industry by "management consultants." These were professional problem solvers who believed that something called "fact-based analysis" could make any business work better. They placed no stock in understanding how a specific business worked, and in fact made an ignorance of it a virtue. That said, they gained considerable influence in many of the leading banks because the financial industry found itself in a genuine crisis at the beginning of the 1980s. Three problems were closing in on it.

First, the capital markets had already replaced most of the banks' safe, high-quality lending. Banks had to find new customers and markets or become obsolete.

Second, U.S. regulators and their international counterparts were insisting on higher capital requirements for banks. At the same time, institutional investors were demanding higher and higher returns—that is profits—on that capital.

Third, the U.S. banks were still in a straitjacket of state and federal regulations that forbade them to merge or open branches across state lines or engage in the securities businesses that were eating their lunch.

The question was, what could U.S. banks do? The answer seemed to be to create new markets, and new "products," at a pace never before seen.

Looking back, people will see the 1982 to 2007 quarter century as a wild flowering of creativity in the financial world. If things turn out as badly as it looks like they might, people will also wonder why somebody didn't stop it in its tracks. The answer is, in part, because "innovation" is genuinely viewed as a good thing in our culture—change is a good word. The other answer is that this was a quarter century of remarkably benign financial circumstances. Above all, it was a great party, and lots of people got very rich.

BANKS DISCOVER CONSUMER LENDING

The early 1980s witnessed something that has been called the retail banking revolution. This started in the United States and spread to the United Kingdom and other rich countries. Traditionally, banks only looked to consumers like you and me for deposits. Classic banking turned our OPM into "working capital" for business and industry. Lending money to consumers was always left to retailers, finance companies, and savings banks. There were exceptions, like a loan secured by a new car or an overdraft line on a current account secured by a steady income and a lien on a house. However, as a rule, prudent banks never lent money for personal consumption, only to smooth out household cash flow. The reason for this is obvious: Anyone who spends more money than they make will, as Mr. Micawber reminds us in *David Copperfield*, ends up miserable. Any banker who lends for consumption risks another form of misery.

Yet, starting in the 1980s, lending money to consumers for consumption became the most profitable and fastest growing business in U.S. banking. This was possible because banks were able to create specialized consumer businesses organized around "products" like mortgages, unsecured revolving credit, and home-equity loans. These product businesses were national in scope. A bank can attach a revolving credit line to a payment card or a home equity lien without having any other relationship with a customer. Mortgages are much the same. Bank's inability to own other branches or have deposit relationships with borrowers suddenly didn't matter because these products could be sold and managed using mail, phone, and, later, the Internet to reach customers.

What *did* matter was the ability to run these product businesses with efficient industrial processes, what economists call "economies of scale." A big consumer credit issuer can analyze millions of potential target customers and generate millions of mail pieces and process millions of applications at far less cost per customer than can a local bank. These businesses required investments in technology to achieve this sort of throughput, investments only big players could make. This meant that these businesses soon became concentrated nationally.

THE ROLE OF TECHNOLOGY

It is often asserted that technology causes change. It is more accurate to say that it *allows* things to *be* changed. Figuring out how to make good use of a technology is a lot harder than inventing it. The retail banking revolution was made possible because a few clever bankers figured out how to string together some rather simple technical advances that became widespread in the 1980s. Banks themselves invented nothing.

The first key technology was computers that they could store and run number-crunching programs on millions of pieces of data about millions of consumers. Computers had been used in bank accounting and payment processing since the 1960s, but only in the 1980s were they clever enough to make it possible to use math in place of personal judgment to determine whether or not a customer could be trusted with money.

THE LOST ART OF CREDIT

In the old days, bankers, including myself at the time, were taught something called "credit." It was more art than science, and required experience as well as training. Credit rested on a sort of rule Bagehot would have endorsed called the five "Ps": First, *People,* their overall character and standing in the community. Knowing and trusting your customer was fundamental. Second, *Purpose,* the use the money would be put to, especially whether it would generate wealth or income. Third, *Payment,* a clear understanding of where the money to repay the loan would actually come. Fourth, *Protection,* what collateral or guarantees could secure the loan if *Payment* fell through for any reason. Fifth, *Perspective,* did the proposition of this customer borrowing this amount of money pass the test of common sense? If all of this sounds a bit restrictive and old school, yes it was. But bankers felt they had a duty of care toward their customers and communities to prevent the imprudent use of credit. It was a duty that mere moneylenders like consumer finance companies and pawn shops didn't have, but there was a clear distinction understood by bankers and their customers between bankers and money lenders. You didn't go to your bank for a second mortgage just to finance your dream vacation.

YOUR CREDIT SCORE

Computer credit scoring made the five Ps obsolete for consumer lending. Banks could use well-established statistical techniques to develop the mathematical probability that a given individual would default on a loan for a certain amount. This probability of non-payment is reduced to the number you know as your credit score. If you are in the 800s, there is very little probability you will not repay me. If you are in the 500s, I should not lend you money. Credit scores depend on the law of large numbers, meaning the more individuals in the statistical base, the more accurate the predictions. This is why big independent credit bureaus like TRW grew up so the same type of data on credit use from as many lenders as possible could be assembled on as many consumers as possible. Another independent industry grew up around the building and selling of so-called risk models, the statistical engines that did the number-crunching. Fair Isaac pioneered the FICO score, the number that more or less determines how much credit, if any, a lender gives you and at what terms.

THE SUB-PRIME TEMPTATION

This is where another word you hear tossed around in the news: Sub-prime. This is a euphemism for "This person *may* be trouble." Some banks use terms like near-prime or simply non-prime, but it really comes down to a borrower who would not have passed the 5P test in the good old days. The reason you hear the word a lot today is that until not so long ago, mainstream banks and mortgage companies just said no to sub-prime applications for credit. As bank consumer lending boomed, the business became very competitive. Anyone with a good FICO score could expect to receive tons of unsolicited offers for credit cards, home equity loans and lines of credit, mortgages, and mortgage refinance through the mail. In some upscale zip codes, the banks carpet bombed whole populations with offers. Eventually, the law of diminishing returns set in with a vengeance. Fewer and fewer credit-worthy people would respond to offers. The market became very competitive and rates fell since every lender depended on the same credit scores to identify "good" borrowers. As banks ran out of safe borrowers, they began to search for safe ways to lend money to unsafe customers. Some began to tip toe into the "sub-prime" market by developing better and better risk models. These, however, were easily replicated by rivals since everybody has access to the same computers and the same statistical tools. To lend money profitably to anyone with a pulse, a new thing was required. That thing turned out to be the fatal blooming of financial innovation known as "structured finance."

ENTER STRUCTURED FINANCE

The whole world of structured finance is based on one simple idea or insight. When investors buy a financial instrument of the type we describe in Chapter Two, they are always putting down money today to get more money tomorrow. In finance-speak, they are buying a future cash flow. The traditional financial instruments are, as we saw, simply accidents of history that stood the test of time. The basic conceit of structural finance is that entirely new, customized financial instruments could be manufactured by "slicing and dicing" the cash flows from any type of traditional loan. For example, any consumer loan carries a certain risk of default. The borrower's credit score should predict this risk with some statistical certainty. If a bank holds that loan on its books, it needs to put aside a cushion of capital— spare money—against the risk of non-payment. The risk is typically too large for sub-prime borrowers to be profitable unless they pay such sky high rates of interest that consumer advocates, Congress, and state attorney generals go nuts over them.

However, if a large pool of sub-prime loans are put together in a legal entity outside the bank, the possibilities of making money are endless. First, the chances of all the loans in such a pool going south at the same time can be proved statistically to be quite small, especially if they come from many regions of the country. Second, the future cash flows can be sliced into risk buckets called "tranches" in finance-speak. Tranches can run from the very-risky to the not-too-risky. Bonds based on likely future cash flows from each tranche can be created, each aimed at a different type of investor. Cash flows can be "credit enhanced" by a variety of techniques including giving first claim on the cash going into the pool to some classes of bonds or obtaining external insurance and guarantees. The bank putting together the pool may also retain the worst of the loans or agree to absorb the losses up to a point on other tranches.

CUSTOM-MADE SECURITIES

It all sounds complicated, but what is really going on is that custom financial instruments are being built for specific types of end investors—high-interest risky ones for hedge funds and speculators, safe and highly rated ones for pension funds. In fact, the whole point of a "structure" is to artificially create a certain bond rating. The top independent credit rating agencies were central to the whole process. To sell the financial instruments at all, the issuers had to get a bond rating from Moody's, Standard & Poor's, or Fitch. These firms started out rating the quality of bonds and commercial paper a century or more ago and effectively enjoy a monopoly. Institutional investors are often limited by these company's published ratings in terms of what investments their boards or regulators will let them buy. However, the rating agencies are paid by the issuer seeking the rating. It is as if your kids paid the teacher who gave them their report card grades. As a result, structuring and credit enhancing of an asset pool is designed so that at least one highly rated security emerges from the mess, along with other securities that are at least rated high enough to be marketed. In other words, the structured finance folks start with the rating they need and work backwards, adding as many bells and whistles to the structure as necessary to get the needed rating. The rating in turn is somewhat determined by the kind of investors to whom they hope to sell the stuff.

THE FATAL FLAWS

Stepping back, the wisdom of hindsight tells us this was always going to end in tears. Everything about it was just plain wrong. First, banks, or rather specialist consumer businesses, many of which were not owned by banks, no longer had reason to adhere to old fashioned credit standards. FICO scores would do fine because the structuring industry used them in its models. It scarcely mattered to consumer lenders because they were only doing "origination" of credit. At most, they might have to warehouse their loans until they could be sold as a bundle. Holding a loan until maturity—actually depending on it to be paid back—was old fashioned.

TOO MANY COOKS

Second, the process of structuring consumer credit itself depended on a complex machinery that had too many moving pieces. The loans had to be pooled in a special-purpose legal entity. This allowed the bonds to be issued at ratings that reflected the "structure" rather than the underlying credit of the consumers. It also in theory removed the risk of the loans from the balance sheets of the "originators." These structures required the borrowing of money from the commercial paper market or from banks. Lending to these special-purpose "vehicles" became a business in its own right. The more these entities could borrow, the more loans they could buy from the originators.

The structurers were not regulated banks but investment banks that could borrow much more on their capital than a bank could. The more "leverage" they could create from borrowed money, the higher the return on their own capital. The rating agencies made rating the structures their most profitable line of business since they too had a seat at the table. So did armies of lawyers who put complex documentation together around the structures to meet regulatory requirements.

A little known kind of specialist insurance company called a monoline also got in on the act. These outfits started out providing guarantees of the interest payments on municipal bonds. This was a safe and simple business that helped local governments borrow at lower interest rates. Soon, these companies got into structured finance, along with other specialist insurers that had added guarantees to traditional mortgages. With strong balance sheets, these firms could put an insurance "wrapper" around a pool or tranche of mortgages or other consumer loans to improve the ratings of the bonds issued by the special-purpose vehicle. For a long time, this was a profitable business that appeared low risk for the monolines. The process also fed a small army of accountants, modeling specialists and other consultants, software developers, and academics. In fact, structured finance is probably the first business to make hundreds of math PhDs and other "quants," as the bankers called them, seriously rich.

THE PITCH MEN

Unfortunately, the business was not being run by math geniuses. Ultimately it was being run by bond salesmen. This is the third problem with structured finance. There was more money in selling instruments that were anything but "easily saleable and easily intelligible" than in selling plain vanilla equity and debt. This is not to say that the bond salesmen were deliberately attempting to defraud widows and orphans. The buy-side investors that the sell-side bond salesmen faced off with were hungry for "yield." They were also under pressure. Pension funds, college endowments, mutual funds, and insurance companies all had made big promises of future income. For the most part, these promises were made to you and me. During a twenty-five-year period of relatively low inflation and interest rates, so-called fixed income investors needed to put juice in their portfolios. Plain vanilla bonds issued by governments and large corporations weren't cutting it. Equities were too dangerous, as the dot.com boom and bust of the 1990s clearly proved; besides, many institutions were strictly limited in how much of their funds they could put into stock markets. Enter the bond salesman in his Armani suit and a pitch book giving the answer to an institutional investor's prayers.

FAITH IN RATINGS

The most beautiful thing about structured products was you could buy a nice fat yield without understanding what the darn thing really did or how it worked. The pitch man with his pitch book probably couldn't explain it himself if you put a gun to his head. Explaining was a small part of his job. The products could be sold on yield alone because everybody in the market took the rating agencies very seriously, even the regulators. So if a complex structured bond was rated AAA and yielded a much higher rate of interest than a garden variety AAA corporate bond, buying it made perfect sense. If you couldn't trust the rating agencies, who could you trust? Once a few big institutions were seen to buy a new type of "product," everyone piled in to make more of the stuff. As the supply of one "product" increased, its novelty value to investors eroded. Sales became harder, and profit margins slid. So the sales forces of the big banks and investment banks that did the structuring kept up a steady drum beat demanding new product to sell.

The pace of innovation in reality was driven by end-investor demand—from people like you and me—to get more for our investments. This was in turn translated into pressure on the institutions handling our investments and pension funds. The buy-side institutions in turn demanded new and better yielding "products" and ideas from the sell-side houses. This created tremendous pressures on the structuring specialists, the quants and nerds, to come up with new innovations. Rivalry between banks meant that any new product was almost certainly going to become a low-margin commodity within a year or less. So the pressure to come up with new product eroded all vestiges of cautious "test and learn" experimentation. It was like putting aircraft into mass production before properly testing them. Banks began selling "products" before they had worked out all the accounting or thought through all the risks. It was innovate or die in the minds of many.

THE ILLUSION OF SCIENTIFIC RISK MANAGEMENT

This brings us to the fourth thing that was deeply wrong in the whole world of structured finance and securitization—the death of common-sense risk management. Until about a generation ago, few bankers were open to innovation for the same reasons Bagehot taught. The ways of lending money safely are simple, obvious, and admit no variation. If top management in a bank did not understand a new financing technique, they rejected it out of hand. After all, other people's money was at risk.

Something big happened in the 1980s to change all that. Banks became seized with a superstitious belief that complex mathematical models could better manage financial risk and return than human judgment. This thinking went well beyond the FICO score or the models used by the rating agencies to "stress test" default probabilities. Banks came to believe that they could design and implement data-driven "scientific" risk systems. The key concepts were "value at risk" or VAR and "risk adjusted return on capital" or RAROC. The basic idea was simple. Every loan, trading position, or operating exposure such as fraud or computer systems failure involved risks that could be identified and quantified with some precision across the whole institution. Risks were quantified by measuring the potential gap between the expected income from a loan or investment and the income actually received if things went wrong. What these were and their probability was largely a matter of analyzing the historical performance of similar investments and loans. Probability depends on history, usually pretty short-term history, to predict likely outcomes. It does not consider what are called "long-tail events," otherwise know as "black swans."

If you shoot golf in the low eighties for ten years, the statistical probability is that your next golf score will be in the same range. The chance of your making several holes in one or being hit by lightning exists, but these are "extreme events" on the long tail of the mathematical bell curve of probabilities. These by definition cluster around the average in the middle of the curve. The problem is that the extreme events at the very edges of probability can be hugely destructive. Events like Pearl Harbor and the attacks of 9/11 were considered extremely remote by experts until they actually happened.

TRIUMPH OF RISK SCIENCE

VAR models were designed to allow banks to control the risks they were taking in a very scientific and rigorous manner. Until the events that began to unfold in the summer of 2007, almost everyone considered the mathematical measurement and modeling of risk to be a great advance over the traditional judgment-based approach. Banks and investment banks spent tens of millions of dollars on computer systems that allowed the exposure to risk of every line of business, down to loan portfolios and trading positions, to be calculated. Many banks were capable of producing daily reports that summed up the value at risk of the entire institution on a daily basis. These VAR reports were reviewed by top management and taken seriously by them and the risk management committees of their boards. Regulators, including the Bank for International Settlements, which represented the central banks of the world's advanced economies, endorsed this approach to risk.

So why did all this fail so miserably? The heart of the matter is that, as bankers knew well in Bagehot's day, extreme events cannot be modeled or predicted from historical data. The world is far too random to be reduced to elegant mathematics. A global market meltdown impacting every type of financial market and instrument has never occurred with such speed and ferocity as happened in the fall of 2008, not even in the 1930s. Models built on history don't help us when events are this extreme. Bankers and regulators used to know that it was dangerous to rule out catastrophic market events. That is why banks are required by regulators to leave aside enough liquid investments and cash to act as shock absorbers against unexpected losses. Regulators always want more capital in banks. In fact, even before formal bank regulation began, the boards of many banks made a point of having a large capital to attract customers.

INVESTOR DEMAND VERSUS CAPITAL CUSHION

However, most of the world's largest banks are publicly traded companies with demanding investors, the institutions that hold our pensions and insurance policies. We demand that our savings make money for us, so the folks who manage our money demand that stocks they invest in have good earnings. Banks and other financial services companies are only one of many industry sectors. They compete for investor dollars with each other. During the long bull market of 1982 through 2004, the bar for return on capital was set pretty high, 15% or so being table stakes for many investors.

As a result, banks became much more disciplined about measuring and managing their returns on capital. The motivation was simple. The new game of national consumer lending businesses demanded scale and expensive technology, as did all the sales and trading businesses that had grown up around it. Banks believed they needed to get bigger. The legal and regulatory barriers to mergers within states and within whole regions were falling fast. In the financial market ecology, the big banks were going to be those with the ability to eat other banks. Market capitalization—the total stock market price of all the shares in a company—decided who got to eat whom. If one bank of comparable size had stock worth much more to investors than a second bank, it could buy the second bank using stock instead of cash. Management in the target bank might not have liked it, but boards of public companies are required by law to accept offers that are in the interests of the shareholders. Being offered $50 stock for $25 stock is hard to say no to for any board.

THE RAROC CULT

Being eaten is as painful for a bank as anyone else. Being an eater of banks brought much larger salaries and bonuses to top management. These things tend to focus the mind. A new "science" of capital management grew up, again aided and abetted by management consultants and the statistical tools we have already seen. The big idea was something called risk adjusted return on capital or RAROC. This was basically a way of measuring what every dollar of capital used by a bank to support its businesses returned to the shareholders after adjusting for risk, that is, the probable losses. Other tools and concepts like shareholder value added or SVA also got traction. In theory, if a bank took capital out of a business with low-risk adjusted returns and put it into businesses with high-risk adjusted returns, its overall return on shareholder funds should be higher. So would its position on the banking food chain. It seemed like a good idea at the time.

In fact, RAROC was riddled with the same problems as VAR in terms of reliance on risk models. It also had serious problems of defining exactly where to draw the lines around different businesses within a bank and how to divvy up shared income and expense. Remember, bank intermediation had always been one simple business with many customers providing OPM on one end and borrowing it on the other. The concepts of "products" and "lines of business" with their own profit-and-loss statements and their own chunk of capital was largely an invention of management consultants. The whole thing was somewhat artificial and arbitrary. For example, in Bagehot's time, joint-stock banks thought of each branch as a business unit. A good branch was a profitable one because it took in enough deposits and made enough loans to cover its costs.

In the new world of banking, the branch would be simply a "cost of distribution" for a bunch of "products" like loans, mortgages, credit cards, savings deposits, checking accounts, and CDs. How much should each of these "businesses" pay to the branch system of the bank? How much should they contribute to the core accounting and transaction systems in the bank's computers or the data processing staff? There are no easy answers for any of these things. Again, fancy math gives the illusion of precision when it really depends on piles of assumptions and rules of thumb. Anyone in science or engineering who tries to model complex systems knows this, though few admit it out loud. The wonder of banking since the 1980s is that a simple business was made into a very complex system in the hope that it could be managed "by the numbers."

THE SECURITIZATION IMPERATIVE

RAROC calculations made one thing very clear to the bank managements: If you want a high-risk adjusted return on capital, don't do stuff that needs a lot of capital. Since bank balance sheet intermediation demands big capital buffers, lending money was by definition less capital efficient than "originating" loans for the structured finance sausage machine. Fee income did not eat up capital, so growing fee-based businesses like payments and asset management were good things. Overall, anything that transferred what are called "risk-assets" off the bank balance sheet was a good thing. So was anything that allowed risk itself to be stripped out of a financial instrument and sold to others. This is where the otherwise benign derivatives we saw in the last chapter went bad.

DERIVATIVES GONE BAD

"Good" derivatives allow buyers and sellers to hedge their risks in a market where everyone knows what is being traded. In other words, the things being traded are "easily saleable and easily intelligible." Markets in foreign exchange, stocks, bonds, and even interbank deposits all lend themselves to parallel derivatives markets. When the underlying instruments are hard to sell and impossible to understand things get very sticky. That is where structured finance rears its ugly head. The more complex a deal, the more its moving parts, the harder it is to value. If the underlying instrument that gives the derivatives its value is itself impossible to value, things can get very ugly.

For example, when you hear the words "toxic assets" or "troubled assets" on the evening news, most of what you are hearing about are structured finance instruments based on pools of mortgages, "collateralized mortgage obligations" or CMOs. These proved such a success in getting mortgages off the books of lenders that the same structuring process was used to get business loans off the books. These collateralized loan obligations, or CLOs, were joined by collateralized debt obligations, or CDOs, that pooled corporate debt. Obviously, such instruments lose value very quickly when the value of the underlying mortgages, loans, and bonds becomes questionable. Basically, they become "unsaleable." Buying and selling makes prices, so without such transactions, there is no way to put a value on these instruments.

DERIVATIVES PILED ON DERIVATIVES

All this would be bad enough, but it gets worse. Banks used derivatives to hedge their bets on many of these structured credit deals. At the extreme end of this complexity within complexity were so-called *synthetic* CDOs. These structures did not even own a pool of real assets like bonds or loans. Instead, they used something called a credit default swap or CDS to gain "credit exposure" to pools of assets. "Credit exposure" is finance-speak for getting paid to take risk. Without going into detail, a credit default swap is a derivative in which the seller of protection on a loan or bond gets paid a fee and ongoing premium by the owner of the instrument. If a pre-defined event of default happens, the swap is triggered. The seller takes the bond, and the buyer gets paid its full value.

The credit default market is the largest single derivatives market in the financial world, with contracts outstanding amounting to $45 trillion on the eve of the financial crisis. Despite financial geniuses like the editors of *60 Minutes* denouncing it as a form of gambling, it is a perfectly legitimate way for investors and lenders to hedge their bets against the default of a major corporation or country. Only when mixed into something as complex as structured credit does this sort of derivative spell trouble.

What large financial institutions were able to do was move debt off their books by pooling other financial institutions in CDO structures, and then buy synthetic CDOs that gave them the credit exposure and the income. This clever structure allowed banks to offload assets from balance sheets and reduce their capital requirements. This reduced their regulatory capital requirements, thus improving RAROC. However, when the underlying debt began to deteriorate, the synthetic CDOs suddenly became toxic assets that actually magnified the potential losses the banks faced. This sounds complicated because it was, too complicated for banks and their regulators to really have a grip on. When the music stopped, many banks found themselves with exposures they could not measure and manage to instruments and structures they didn't fully understand. The markets simply stopped functioning.

THE ILLUSION OF PROGRESS

It is important to understand that nobody set out to create a global crisis, let alone do anything dishonest. Financial innovation was all about getting more credit into the hands of consumers, making more income using less capital, and turning what had been concentrated risks off the books of banks into securities that could be traded between and owned by professional investors who could be expected to look after themselves. Like much of the "progress" of the last century, it was a matter of replacing common sense and tradition with science. The models produced using advanced statistics and computers were designed by brilliant minds from the best universities. At the Basle Committee, which set global standards for bank regulation to be followed by all major central banks, the use of statistical models to measure risk and reliance on the rating agencies were baked into the proposed rules for capital adequacy.

The whole thing blew up not because of something obvious like greed. It failed because of the hubris, the fatal pride, of men and women who sincerely thought that they could build computer models that were capable of predicting risk and pricing it correctly. They were wrong.

4
▼

HOW WE GOT HERE

Henry Ford famously said that history is bunk. In fact, history is essential to understanding the present and the real options for the future. Politicians and so-called intellectuals typically think that the institutions we use in our daily lives such as schools, hospitals, and banks are basically mechanical contrivances or "systems" that can and should be changed for the better. All we need to do is get a bunch of big-brain Ivy League types in a room, pass some laws, and spend lots of money. This view partially reflects arrogance and ignorance, but also self-interest. Making the world as we find it work better is too much like hard work.

REAL HISTORY

In his writing about money and banking, Walter Bagehot, who understood his subject better than anyone before or since, was careful to acknowledge the very limited scope for changing or reforming the British financial markets based on his ideas. He insisted that we need to accept the cards we have been dealt by "real history" as opposed to the "conjectural history" of our institutions. Conjectural history is our human instinct to look at how institutions like banks work today and assume that somehow they were created for these purposes instead of being the messy result of accidents of "real" history.

The Real History of Public Education

A non-financial example of "real" versus "conjectural" history is public education in the United States. You probably think of secular government schools as a fundamental invention of American democracy. The "real" history of education in America is far different. In the early days of the republic, many states had an "established" church supported by taxes. In New England, the Congregational Church was established and provided education through its colleges (Harvard and Yale) and "common schools" that were open to all. Eventually, most states dumped their established church, with Connecticut in 1818 and Massachusetts in 1833 being the last to do so. However, local tax support for essentially Protestant "common schools" was continued under the rubric of "public education."

Political support for public education grew largely in reaction to the great Irish immigration of the 1840s. Americans feared that Catholicism would erode their purely Protestant culture. Massachusetts passed the first laws to make school attendance compulsory in 1851, largely to force Catholic kids into Protestant schools. Public education gradually acquired a mission to indoctrinate children to suit political rather than religious agenda, and hence rituals like the Pledge of Allegiance. Public schools everywhere remained basically Protestant. Only in the 1960s did this hostility to one religion morph into the rejection of all religion from tax-supported schools. This rejection was largely justified by an implied "conjectural history," including a distorted view of what the Founders intended by the establishment clause and a mythical "wall of separation."

THE CONJECTURAL HISTORY TRAP

A similar "real" versus "conjectural" history lens can be applied to just about every institution in our economic, social, and political life that we take for granted. The point of "real history" is that institutions are organic, not mechanical. Often they end up serving ends they were never designed to serve. In fact, they were never designed, period. They happened for reasons nobody remembers. What survives the test of time may not be ideal but it works. People who try to reform or change our institutions rarely appreciate this and almost always make a mess of things for that very reason.

THE REAL HISTORY OF BANKING AND FINANCE

The following is a quick survey of financial "real history," the accidents of history that led the global financial market and national banking systems to assume their current form. This history will help you understand how the seeds of the current debacle were planted and how limited the options for real reform actually are.

How the Italians Invented Banking and Finance

In Chapter Two, we met some Italian bankers financing the wool trade in medieval London and Milan by discounting bills of exchange. The Italians invented, in one form or another, almost all the financial institutions and instruments that we have discussed before Columbus sailed. Like Columbus, modern finance is generally believed to have been born in the seafaring republic of Genoa.

There is a good reason for this. The Mediterranean was the highway for trade in valuable commodities like silk and spices between Western Europe and the East. Italy's geography gave enterprising Italian merchants an inside track, which they used to grow rich by expanding trade over the Alps and deep into Asia. They were remarkably free to do business. The Italian peninsula had no effective central government between the fall of Rome in 476 and the final unification of 1871. While many parts of Italy did suffer from local tyrants or foreign conquerors, in other areas, merchants and traders were able to establish self-governing "communes." These developed into republics inspired by ancient Roman civic and legal traditions. Genoa was one of the first of these commercial republics, along with city states like Venice, Pisa, Florence, and Siena. These republics were sensibly designed to promote commerce and protect citizens from government abuse and foreign enemies. Their powers were limited. This meant that they had to borrow money from their citizens when a big project or a war demanded it rather than just grab resources the way tyrants and kings did.

PUBLIC FINANCES

These republics actually had to pay back the money they borrowed from the public and keep honest books. Keeping good financial books is a big deal. In Genoa, for example, public officials were chosen by lottery and served only one year, at the end of which they had to give a detailed accounting of the state finances.

Orderly public finances allowed the Genoese state to develop a very sophisticated public debt market, starting with many unique single-purpose loans but evolving into a single public debt represented by uniform tradable government bonds. In other words, we see the "contract in a box" in action well before 1400. Buying and selling financial instruments flourished and with it innovations like compounding interest on investments.

Citizens and charitable institutions found that they could invest in government debt for current and future income, legacies or endowments, or just to discount or sell back debt to the state or other investors when they needed cash. The Genoese debt market also attracted foreign investors. The public debt of Genoa expanded and contracted with military and civil needs over the centuries, but it was always tied to tax revenues. The Genoese also developed so-called sinking-funds, specific tax revenues explicitly applied to pay down the public debt from time to time. Their public debt market was a pioneer of market intermediation everywhere.

The Public Banks

The Genoese public debt also led to the creation of the first really big balance sheet intermediary. Basically, in 1407, a group of rich merchants did a deal with the state to consolidate its debts into a single loan at a lower interest rate in return for certain privileges that included not only collecting taxes and managing the income but opening a public bank, a bank that took deposits from the public. The Bank of Saint George, which opened in 1408, was only the second such bank in Europe (the first public bank was started by Catalan merchants in Barcelona in 1401) and did most of the stuff banks do today. You could open a current account, transfer money to other accounts, obtain overdraft credit, discount bills, and take out funds in hard money. The Bank of Saint George became the hub of all commerce in Genoa and, through opening branches, the places controlled by Genoa. It even administered Genoese territorial outposts in places like Cyprus.

Public banks and public debt management were closely aligned, since the cash flow from the debt management operation gave the bank extra resources to lend while at the same time attracting deposits. Other Italian republics also developed public debt funds called the "monte." This literally meant a mountain or big pile of money. The citizens of states like Florence, not all of them rich by any means, could safely invest their spare cash in the loans of the monte, which were the equivalent of today's U.S. Treasury Bonds. Like that in Genoa, several public debt refinancing operations also gave birth to public banks. The Monte dei Paschi di Siena, founded by the magistrates of that city in 1472, is still in business and is now one of the largest banking groups in Italy.

Public versus Private Banks

In the 1400s and 1500s, a split emerged between private bankers, who had evolved from money changers and merchants in commercial cities, and public banks that were sponsored by the state in return for managing public debt. It is no accident that the great private banking houses of this time either used their loot to take over the state (the Medici family of bankers took over the Florentine Republic and became the Dukes of Tuscany; see Niall Ferguson's 2008 book *The Ascent of Money* for their story) or were forced by kings and princes to lend money that was never repaid (the famous Fuggers of Augsburg, German bankers, who were ruined by deadbeat governments). Governments and money make a toxic combination, as we will see in the next chapter. Left to their own devices, governments will take every red cent of private wealth they can lay their hands on in the name of the greater good. A public bank that borrows from private citizens on behalf of the government is relatively safe because the government will want to keep on its good side so it can keep on borrowing. Wealthy private bankers are fair game.

The reason this split is important is that while the idea of purely private, "free" banking is attractive in principle to free market advocates, "real" history tells us that banks and governments almost always end up leaning on each other. The picture isn't always pretty, but "real" history tells us we have to live with some form of government role in banking and finance. The "real" history of how the banks and financial markets came into existence beyond Italy demonstrates this.

FINANCE CROSSES THE ALPS

The great driver of early banking was trade, especially high-stakes, long-distance trade where big profits could be made by the lucky and the bold. Up until 1492, Europe's trade flowed through Italy, but then it began to shift to the high seas beyond the Mediterranean. The commercial republics that invented finance went into decline. The future belonged to the Atlantic world.

MONEY AND POWER

The great nations of early modern Europe—France, Spain, Holland, and England—were born through their wars with each other and through racing to build trade and empire in Asia and the New World. Most of the time, these countries were broke. Unless coerced or robbed, their merchants and bankers were not stupid enough to lend them money. Governments needed to get their hands on big globs of money to fight wars and build empires and maybe the odd palace without busting their subjects with taxes.

FINANCIAL MARKETS

Sir Thomas Gresham solved the problem for Queen Elizabeth's England by importing the Italian notion of selling government debt in an open air London market where people bought wooden stocks. The government debt contracts became known as government stock. That is where the name stock market comes from. Soon stock was not just sold, it was traded. Political turmoil or wars could shake confidence in government stock. So could issuing more stock than people wanted to buy. Once people began trying to make bets—that is, speculate—on future prices, a real debt market with buyers and sellers developed. This happened quickly because London was a trading city and Londoners were used to speculating—betting—on the future value of commodities like grain and wool. Debt was just something new to swap. Because London was so rich and the English state did better than its rivals at war and empire, the London stock market became a big success. Only Amsterdam could rival it, again as the center of a successful trading empire that had adopted Italian financial practices, including a great public bank in 1609.

Success at war and sound public finance proved mutually reinforc-ing. England beat out Spain, France, and Holland in over two centu-ries of nearly constant war between the early 1600s and the early 1800s because of one thing: Money. England managed to put into use far greater sums of money than its rivals because it was far more credible at managing its public debt. As a result, it got to create the modern commercial and political world in its own image.

JOINT-STOCK COMPANIES

The global struggle for empire also caused the English and Dutch to develop the joint-stock company. Lou Dobbs informs us that "out-sourcing" is a very bad thing. Actually, for most of history, govern-ments outsourced just about everything, largely because of lack of money. The English, the Dutch, and the French got rich, private citi-zens to do things by selling them public offices and monopolies.

Some things, however, were too big and risky for any individual to undertake. The first joint-stock companies were organized as trading companies to colonize the New World and Asia. Since the govern-ment wanted to control its colonies, such companies needed a charter from the crown. To make that charter worth a lot, it provided the holder with a monopoly on trade. Raising enough money to set up a colony was no small matter, but a monopoly charter helped close the sale with investors. The Virginian Company, the Dutch West India Company, the Dutch East India Company, the Hudson's Bay Com-pany, the East India Company, the Massachusetts Bay Company, and scores of other monopoly joint-stock companies were set up in the 1600s.

A WORLD OF RISK

European world domination was driven by joint-stock companies up to the middle of the nineteenth century. While not what we think of as a modern public company—i.e., the East India Company had its own ships, armies, and governed much of India—the early joint-stock company was the model for everything that followed. The investors swapped money for shares in the venture, shares they were free to sell to others. The investors were represented by a board of directors that provided oversight to the paid managers who handled day-to-day business. Shares paid dividends based on the profits of the venture. There was a degree of government oversight because these companies' charters and monopolies could always be revoked or simply not renewed. Famously, Warren Hastings, the East India Company president of Bengal, was impeached by Parliament in 1787 for abuse of power. He got off.

If the venture failed, shareholders only stood to lose the money they put in. If it succeeded, the value of their shares went up, and they could sell at a profit. In the mean time, the board would periodically declare a dividend, so shares were also a source of income. Like government debt or "stock," shares in the great English joint-stock companies soon came to be traded, again because their value went up and down with business and political conditions. In fact, they traded in the same place, the Royal Exchange.

FINANCE LEARNS ENGLISH

Stepping back, in the London of the 1690s, we can already see our modern financial ecology in embryo. A banking system based on bills of exchange was extending credit to merchants. Some merchants morphed into full-time bankers. There was an active market in government stock and the shares of joint-stock companies. Specialized middle men were starting to appear. Bill brokers took bills of exchange to the banks for discount. They traded bills among each other on the floor of the Royal Exchange, a great financial market hall built by Gresham. Stock brokers bought and sold government bonds and shares in companies for clients. They too traded with each other. Every corner of the city had coffee houses where these traders met, drank (not just coffee), and made deals. Even the maritime insurance market started in a coffee house owned by a Mr. Lloyd.

"Conjectural" history would suggest that all these embryo institutions evolved through market forces to produce the bank branch on the corner and the mutual fund companies that advertise during the evening news. "Real" history, however, does not work that way. Today's financial world is the imperfect product of the accidents of history. Some of these things made sense at the time, some less so, but what we have is the sum of stuff that happened. It is what it is.

PAPER MONEY

The first accident was the discovery of paper money and credit. This was a big step. Even the subtle Italians mostly confined themselves to using bills of exchange for payments and credit. However, in the 1640s, the English had a nasty civil war between the king and parliament. London had no public bank, so its merchants stored their hard money—gold and silver—in the Royal Mint, which was protected by the garrison at the Tower of London. Needing cash to raise an army, the king simply "borrowed" money from the mint. This taught people to keep their cash far from the reach of the government.

London had a large guild of goldsmiths. They had strong and safe storage rooms. Many got into the business of holding merchants gold and silver for a fee (bank fees are nothing new). Rather than constantly going to the goldsmiths for coin, merchants began using the paper receipts that the goldsmiths gave them to pay each other. The receipts or notes became private paper money. The holder could always take a note to the goldsmith issuing it and demand gold or silver. But as these notes passed hand to hand, few turned up for cash payment. Goldsmiths quickly figured out that they could issue a lot more notes than the amount of gold and silver they actually held in their storerooms. They used this discovery to make loans to merchants who held accounts with them, charging them interest. They became a new kind of banker, taking deposits in hard money and lending out a far larger amount of paper money. As long as people believed they could swap a note issued by a goldsmith-turned-banker for gold, it was as good as gold.

CENTRAL BANKING

The second accident was, in finance-speak, "central banking," in the form of the Bank of England. This involved yet another war that needed financing. In the so-called Glorious Revolution of 1688, William of Orange was made king of England. How or why isn't important to our story, but the effects of his kingship were. King William, also ruler of Holland, took England into the war that the Dutch had been fighting against France. This required borrowing a lot of money. The English government was already up to its eyeballs in debt. The answer was a version of the Italian public bank, a joint-stock company to take over and manage the public debt of England. This required an especially juicy monopoly. Not only did the Bank of England (1694) get to be the sole banker to the government, but it received a monopoly on joint-stock banking in England and Wales. This monopoly was good for 150 years.

These privileges made it a slam dunk investment, bringing in hard money not only from all over England but also from abroad. This meant that the Bank of England was not only able to lend money to the government in amounts and at rates that other countries couldn't match—Louis XIV lost his war against England and Holland, saying, he who has the last gold coin wins—it also became *the* bank in London. No sounder bank existed or could exist. Bank of England notes were regarded as good as gold. Other banks' note-issue business declined, especially in London. The use of checks, those stripped down bills of exchange we met in the last chapter, began in London around 1660 but expanded as private banknotes declined.

The Bank of England, until it was nationalized in1946, was basically a normal stock company intent on making money for its investors. Its privileges, however, allowed it to compete with other London bankers on completely unfair terms. Since the Bank of England made it difficult to lend by handing out their own banknotes to their customers, the private bankers found it was actually better to keep spare cash—their hard money reserve—in the Bank of England and pay their depositors who wanted cash in Bank of England notes. In doing so, they benefited from the multiplication of money made possible by deposit banking at less risk. Keeping their reserve of hard money in the Bank of England allowed each bank to do more lending overall. Managing these reserves allowed the Bank of England to learn how to influence the supply and price of credit in the London money market. Modern central banks like our Federal Reserve System were all modeled on the Bank of England.

CLEARING HOUSES

The third happy accident was the clearing house. The Genoese can rightly claim to have invented central clearing and settlement of bills of exchange centuries before the English did. As much as half the trade in Europe was settled up at quarterly exchange fairs the Genoese conducted for this purpose in key towns across Europe. These allowed bankers and merchants to exchange very large amounts of payments for one net sum. Conjectural history would suggest that the English adopted Genoese practice.

The real history is far different. As deposit banking using checks and drafts grew in response to the Bank of England banknote monopoly, the private banks came to employ a small army of bank messengers. These men and boys walked from bank to bank with bills and checks for payment, each bank sending out its own employees several times a day in all kinds of weather. These guys were not stupid and by the mid-1700s had figured out that they could save a lot of walking (and enjoy some on-the-job drinking) by meeting at fixed times in the same tavern to exchange their "bank mail." The pub in question became the first London clearing house, a sort of club of bank messengers who knew and trusted each other. It seems to have taken the bankers who employed them a while to catch on, but when they did (around 1750), they simply bought the tavern and turned it into a private club with its own committee to make and enforce rules. By 1773, the London Clearing House was a going concern with its own building. The rules of the club explicitly excluded joint-stock banks, which at the time only meant the Bank of England.

SELF-REGULATION

The fourth happy accident is market self-regulation. Clearing house rules were the first whiff of "law and order" in the rapidly growing world of London finance. The Bank of England Act of 1694 and the subsequent Bank Charter Act of 1844 only gave duties and monopoly rights to that specific bank. It said nothing about banks in general or their regulation. In English legal terms, a banker was basically any person or firm that other banks recognized as being one. the law didn't say what a bank *could* do or *had* to do. This vacuum was filled by the clearing house. With clearing house membership, a private London bank could attract deposit money from "country" banks elsewhere in Britain and from overseas banks needing to make payments or discount bills in London. Therefore, obtaining and keeping membership in the clearing house was a big deal. Only safe and sound banks could obtain and maintain membership.

This inner club of what came to be know as "clearing banks" fluctuated around a few dozen firms for many years, eventually being reduced to ten or so by the early twentieth century as banks bought each other or merged. The clearing house members in turn influenced the safety and soundness of the numerous "country banks" outside of London. Clearing banks decided whose banknotes they would cash and whose bills they would discount and on what terms. After all, the self-interest of their club demanded that members keep their noses clean and that the banks they did business with did so too. In return for not doing risky or crazy things, the banks in the Clearing House Club could hope for a degree of mutual support from their fellow members in times of financial crisis.

In other words, the clearing house provided the first system of financial regulation. Voluntary self-regulation is not very popular these days. However, the simple fact is that no private clearing house has ever collapsed during a financial crisis. The history of formal regulation is less stellar. The United States has experienced two devastating structural financial crises and several lesser ones since the Federal Reserve was set up. The Northern Rock bank run in England (the first since 1866) happened after the U.K. abolished the old clearing house "club" and took up formal regulation.

LONDON BECOMES MONEY MARKET TO THE WORLD

The result of all these accidents of history was that England became the first national economy based on credit. Nothing really new in finance has been invented since. The building blocks have been simple to use once they actually existed. Bringing them into existence was the challenge. Almost every country adopted or developed local versions of the English credit money machine once its power became obvious.

To sum up these building blocks, take a look at the following:

1. Deposit money in banks becomes the "store of value"—the stuff people swap for other stuff.
2. Deposit money becomes multiplied by banks keeping a safe minimum of hard money in one big bank that is backed up by the government.

3. Banks develop a "payment system" around the hub of a clearing house, making a lot of payments with little use of cash.
4. The clearing house keeps order among the banks and lets its members get deposits and transactions from the banks outside of it.

Put all these blocks together and you have an avalanche effect. Deposits get concentrated in the London clearing banks because that is where you can most easily lend, borrow, and make payments. All these deposits create a "money market," a big pool of money in one place. Once the money market is really big, everyone who needs money goes there for it. Bills of exchange get discounted. Stocks and bonds get traded. So do real stuff, commodities. All these markets need cash to grease the wheels. All need "clearing and settlement." All of this sucks in more money, which through the magic of deposit banking gets multiplied, growing the loan pool.

THE MARKET AND THE PLAYERS EMERGE

If looked at as a map, we see there are a series of circles in which the "inner banks" (the clearing house banks) sit smack in the middle. Off to the side is the Bank of England, which keeps the banks' cash reserves and sets the price of money in the market. In the second circle are the smaller private and "country" banks that need the "inner banks" to pay checks and collect bills for their customers. In the third circle, we see a larger cast of characters who live off the OPM sloshing around the inner banks.

The first and most important are called "bill brokers," who take the risk of discounting bills of exchange using money borrowed short term from the inner banks and the Bank of England. Their day-to-day business keeps the money market turning over. Second are the "accepting houses" or "merchant bankers." These started as big merchant houses so well known that their bills got the best rates. Now they "rent" their good name to less well-known merchants, especially foreigners, by adding their "acceptance"—in effect their guarantee—for a fee.

Almost all merchant bankers had roots outside of England: Rothschild from Frankfurt, Barings from Copenhagen, Hambros from Hamburg, Peabody and Morgan from New England, Brown Brothers from Baltimore. Being international was essential. It gave these firms insider knowledge of which foreign bills were safe to accept. Most of these firms were family businesses in which fathers, sons, and brothers ran key overseas outposts and trusted each other to protect the family name and money. For more on the Rothschilds, who were the greatest practitioners of high finance in history, turn to *The Ascent of Money* or Ferguson's full-scale history, *The Rothschilds.*

THE FIRST INVESTMENT BANKS

The magic of the merchant bankers was that they used very little of their own money to mobilize huge chunks of OPM from the inner banks. They *arranged* financing, mainly in the form of bonds, but did not normally *provide* financing. They did this on a huge scale. As usual, war provided big opportunities. The French Revolution set off over twenty years of more or less constant war in Europe. This forced England and her allies to borrow huge sums of money in the London market. Merchant bankers like Rothschild filled this need and grew immensely wealthy in the process. Baring Brothers raised the money for Jefferson to buy Louisiana from Napoleon and helped finance Latin American independence. Later the Rothschilds advanced the money for Britain to buy the Suez Canal. The great London merchant bankers also financed the huge expansion of world trade and the building of railroads and factories around the globe that marked the long peace of 1815 through 1914.

The number one destination for all this London money was the United States, not Britain or her empire. America was growing in territory, population, and industry at breakneck speed. It had a bottomless appetite for credit and money. What it didn't have, for reasons we will address in the next chapter, was serious banks or financial markets. The merchant bankers brought American opportunity and British money together. They were the gatekeepers of the Great London Loan Pool.

THE STOCK EXCHANGE

This brings us to the fourth circle, the stock exchange. The London Stock Exchange was born in a coffee house called Jonathan's, where anyone who wanted to buy and sell government stock or shares in joint-stock companies could just show up. Like the clearing house, the coffee house became a club in the late 1700s. A stock broker was by definition a member of the club, which decided who was and was not allowed to join. Members had the sole right to trade on the exchange, which was really just a big room. Anybody wanting to buy or sell stock needed to use a stock broker who made money by charging customers fees to make trades.

HIGH STREET BANKING AND HIGH FINANCE

The first joint-stock bank aside from the Bank of England was founded in 1837, and soon many others followed. Bagehot rightly saw this as something of a revolution. From its birth in medieval Italy until about one hundred fifty years ago, banking had only served businesses and the wealthy. Everybody else conducted their lives with cash and barter. Joint-stock banking changed all that. It turned what had been a "handicraft" business run by a handful of partners into a "factory" business employing thousands of workers. In this, it simply imitated the rise of modern industry.

BRANCH BANKING

The key innovation was branch banking, something you and I take for granted. Using money raised in the stock market, the new British joint-stock banks built imposing branches in every large town and suburb. The Scottish banks had invented branches in the 1720s, but nothing on this scale. If you had the minimum deposit required, you could open a current account in one of those branches. With the account came a check book, which allowed you to make payments and borrow money by overdrawing your account. You also got a new professional called your bank manager. The bank manager both provided financial advice and kept you on the financial straight and narrow. None of these ideas were really new—wealthy persons and merchants had run overdrafts at private banks for a long time—but the joint-stock banks made them available to the whole professional and upper middle class as well as businesses of all sizes. The ability to borrow money by writing a check became a part of daily life.

BALANCE SHEET LENDING

This completely changed how banks lent money. As long as the bank manager follows simple rules to the letter, giving a large overdraft to a company or a merchant is not really much more risky than discounting individual bills. It's actually a lot simpler to do. The banker only has to watch your account and "control" the overdraft. The borrower does all the real work with his or her check book. All the banker does is keep an eye on your account overdraft. If you have good collateral and lots of income flowing through your current account, he doesn't need to know the details of your day-to-day business.

From the customers' viewpoint, overdraft lending makes life simpler. They can use their overdraft credit flexibly, smoothing out peaks and valleys in their cash position. The older handicraft model of real-bills banking simply could not compete with this "loan factory" system. Many of the country banks and private banks became joint-stock banks or were bought up by them. As the joint-stock banks got bigger and national in their branch networks, they also developed strong brands with the public. Their checks were accepted everywhere because they had branches everywhere, so it made little sense not to keep your money in one. By 1900 or so, a mere handful of joint-stock banks held the vast majority of deposits in Britain.

This deposit monopoly meant that the joint-stock banks were not dependent on the London money market as private banks and bill brokers had been. For every customer who needed a big overdraft, they had another who kept lots of money in the bank. With big networks of branches up and down the country, some deposit rich and some loan heavy, they in effect ran their own internal money market. The money market remained important, but mainly as a place each big bank could put any extra money to work after adding up internal deposit and loan balances. Collectively, the big joint-stock banks had the majority of both. They controlled the clearing house, which once excluded them. They kept their reserve in the Bank of England, becoming its biggest customers. They funded and provided clearing and settlement for all the other players in the London financial markets. However, the joint-stock banks' hearts were never in the financial markets.

MAIN STREET AND WALL STREET

Around this time, roughly a century ago, a clear, bright line was emerging between "high street" banking and "high finance," what American politicians call "Main Street" and "Wall Street." High Street is British English for what Americans call Main Street. Every large town had branches of all the "big four," as the leading joint-stock banks came to be known. Bank managers were important, respected people in their communities, like doctors and lawyers. They made it their business to know who had money and who ought to be lent money. They shared information and wouldn't dream of poaching each other's customers. They dispensed financial advice and enforced financial discipline on their customers to a degree we cannot imagine. Bank balance sheet intermediation as we know it today really starts with these Victorian English banks and their many clones around the globe.

"High finance" was the business of raising money for both governments and companies, and financing the foreign trade of Britain and other countries. The business occasionally needed the deposit money in the High Street banks to grease the wheels, but that was the only point the two worlds crossed paths. Merchant bankers and brokers raised the money that built industry and railways around the world from the ranks of the rich, which in Britain ranged from old land-owning money to thousands of new family fortunes based on the vastly expanded trade and industry.

INSTITUTIONAL INVESTORS

These businesses also tapped the savings of rapidly growing ranks of industrial workers and middle-class clerks and tradesmen. These people had begun to buy a new financial product called life insurance. Life insurance started out as working men's clubs called friendly societies. Friendly societies pooled small regular payments from their members into a fund to pay for a respectable funeral when a member died. This was a far cry from the fire and casualty insurance policies of the London insurance markets at Lloyds. That insurance was about wealthy property owners sharing the risk of something really bad happening, like a ship sinking. Not all ships sink, but we do all die.

THE HIDDEN BANKERS

Life insurance is not really about risk; it is about saving for the inevitable over many years. People pay in premiums on a regular basis but only get money out upon death. Nobody really asks or understands what the insurers are doing with the money in the meantime. The answer is not a lot different from banking. The life insurance company rents out OPM. In fact, insurers have been called "the hidden bankers" because they really make their living by lending and investing other people's money for more than they paid for it.

There are really only two big differences between banks and life companies. First, banks need to lend for short periods of time (because their depositors can ask for their money at any time), whereas insurers need to invest for long periods of time (because their policy holders will be dying far in the future). Second, banks pay for OPM with services (branches, payments) and interest, whereas insurers pay for OPM by paying claims. Since statistics can do a pretty good job of predicting when people of a certain age and gender will die, insurance is an even simpler way than banking to make money out of OPM.

The friendly society model was quickly copied on an industrial scale. Some insurance companies, indeed most, were originally owned, at least in theory, by their policy holders. Over time, policies were increasingly designed to pay a death benefit to replace income. The Scottish Church started an insurance scheme to provide for the widows of ministers, starting the trend towards a private pensions industry. (Again, Ferguson covers the Scottish roots of life insurance very well.)

By the late nineteenth century, both London and Scotland held big pools of what we now call "institutional money" that simply *had* to earn a predictable amount of money to pay claims and pensions. This pool kept growing as more and more policies were sold (life insurance is always and everywhere sold; people rarely go out and buy it the way they would go out and open a bank account). This was a door to door business, with even the poorest neighborhoods having their own local agents selling small policies and collecting weekly premiums in cash.

This is where the pennies-a-day policy holder and "high finance" came together. The life insurance industry was the first of the "institutional investors" we met in the first chapter. They fed the growth of high finance by bringing into play a large and growing pot of OPM that was looking for long-term income. This was cautious money looking for a steady return. It needed what we today call "fixed income," which means it needed the bond market as much as the bond market needed it. It also needed return on invested money that would cover predicted future cash outlays with a margin for safety and a profit. That meant that just buying U.K. government stock might be good enough for some or even most of their portfolio of investments, but not all.

FINANCE BRIDGES THE ATLANTIC

This is where the vital link with the United States comes in. Because it became the first banking nation, the first industrial nation, and had a vast global trade and empire, Victorian Britain was awash with money. As Bagehot calculated, there was substantially more money available for loans and investments in London in 1870 than in all the rest of the world combined. Because supply and demand sets prices, London interest rates tended to be low. Both institution investors and rich individuals were looking for a better return.

AMERICA THE BORROWER

Few Americans today realize that for most of our history the United States was a "developing county" hungry for foreign credit and capital. As a result, Americans had to pay over the odds for money. Building America with British institutional money was one of the single biggest games in high finance. The prices of U.S. stocks and bonds were on the cover page of the leading British newspaper. High finance also raised money for projects in other countries and for foreign governments, not to mention domestic British companies, but the world of high finance often looked across the Atlantic.

FOREIGN EXCHANGE

Until this point, from about 1870 onwards, the issue of what a national currency was actually worth in terms of another national currency was not a big deal. There was no market in "foreign exchange" separate from the market in foreign bills of exchange. In high finance, the value of a national currency matters a lot. If I buy a U.S. dollar railway bond with U.K. money, the income from that bond is paid in dollars. If the two currencies are not anchored in some pretty fundamental way, I have taken on a new risk. If the dollar loses value relative to the pound, my income in the money I actually use at home falls. If the railway had borrowed in U.K. money, I would avoid this risk, but the railway might not be able to earn enough dollars to buy the pounds needed to pay me. In any case, it would be a lot easier to decide whether to make the investment knowing that the number of dollars needed to buy a pound would not change. Then I would only have to worry about the ability and willingness of the railway to pay its debts.

THE GOLD STANDARD

The answer to this problem was found in another "real history" accident. The world stumbled onto the gold standard. Without the huge pot of money that high finance had put together in London, this probably never would have happened. You don't need a gold standard or any objective yardstick to determine currency values in ordinary trade. For centuries, foreign bills of exchange flowed between financial centers like London and New York. If a merchant in London sold goods to a merchant in New York, the buyer would pay with a "bill on London" in pounds. If a merchant in America sold goods to an English merchant, the English merchant would pay with a bill on New York in dollars, and so on around the world. In the normal course of things, trade is always a two-way street. Lots of people in England would be owed dollars, and lots of people in America would be owed pounds.

However, you can only use your national currency, not a foreign currency, in your own country—try paying for a New York cab ride in U.K. banknotes. This means everybody ultimately needs to convert foreign income into domestic currency. The solution, going back to the Genoese exchange fairs, is to swap foreign currency bills for local currency bills at a market price. If the London market was awash with bills on New York looking for buyers, the price of dollar bills of exchange would naturally fall. If more people in London needed dollar bills of exchange to make payments in New York, their price would rise until the market was in rough balance.

THE FOREIGN EXCHANGE MARKET

The merchant banks and agencies of foreign banks in London made a business of trading foreign bills, as did dealers in Change Alley near the Royal Exchange. The market was simply a reflection of the balance of trade between countries. Countries that bought more than they sold saw the value of their currency fall until they had to buy less. In the process, their goods would get cheaper in the local currency of their trading partner. Then they could sell more, and, with any luck, things balanced out. Where and when there was a serious shortage of bills in a currency, the difference would be made up in hard money— gold and silver. For example, Europeans and Americans bought more from China than they sold there, and shipped large amounts of silver east as a result.

FINANCE GOES GOLD

So, if this natural, self-adjusting "foreign exchange" based on trade flows worked for many centuries, why did the gold standard emerge? The answer lies in yet another accident of "real history." In 1871, a unified German state emerged from the victory of Prussia over France. The new German empire was on day one the strongest country in Europe. Germany had every reason to think that it could and should be top country instead of England. So, it adopted its own version of the Bank of England, the Reichsbank, a gold-backed paper currency monopoly on the English model, the Reichsmark, and laws making it easy to start up joint-stock banks, all within a few years. Since German trade and industry grew rapidly after unification, Germany also became a model for other new powers like Japan and Italy. The gold standard became a sort of "good housekeeping seal of approval" for sound banking and sound economic policies. Between 1871 and 1900, almost every major country went on to the gold standard. America was the last to do so, with the Democratic candidate William Jennings Bryan running against the gold standard in 1896 and 1900. He lost both times.

THE GOLD STANDARD IN PRACTICE

Was the gold standard a good idea? How did it work? Did it work? The "real history" is that the English gold standard was set up to maintain public trust in the Bank of England's note-issue monopoly. However, finance is to a frightening extent a fashion business. England was the world's leading banking, trading, and manufacturing country, and it controlled the world's oceans and had a vast empire that spanned the globe. It was obviously top country. It also had the gold standard. These things had no demonstrable connection. In fact, most of England's position as top country was established long before the gold standard. Facts don't matter in fashion.

The "real history" behind the global move to the gold standard in the late nineteenth century really concerns what we now call "globalization," a combination of free movement of money and free trade. A currency convertible to gold made any country and the businesses within its borders became more attractive for British investors. Even badly managed countries like Imperial China went on the gold standard so they could borrow. The gold standard also reduced risks to companies involved in overseas trade by setting fixed relationships between currencies; for example, a British pound was always worth $5.40 in U.S. money, so a seller of goods in either country knew exactly what the payments he was owed would be worth.

THE FIRST ERA OF GLOBALIZATION

High finance and trade reinforced each other in building a global marketplace. Take railways, which were the high tech business of the time. Railways worldwide were for sixty years the number one industry bankrolled by high finance. The railways then brought U.S., Canadian, and Australian and Russian wheat into a single global market, coordinated by commodity brokers using the telegraph and telephone, new technologies also bankrolled by high finance. The railways in turn fed the growth of the steel industry worldwide, which fed expanded mining for coal and ore. Steel ships drove down the price of ocean freight, allowing yet more everyday products to be bought and sold globally at ever lower prices. And so on. In a word, high finance built the modern world on the back of the gold standard. Between 1871 and the outbreak of World War I in 1914, the human race experienced its greatest single period of economic growth and development, ever. We can't say that the gold standard made this happen, but it certainly helped it happen.

THE MECHANICS OF THE GOLD STANDARD

How did the gold standard work? Basically, it forced countries to live within their means through an automatic adjustment mechanism. Each country set its national currency unit's value in terms of troy ounces of gold. So, in 1900, when Congress put the United States on the gold standard, it specified that a troy ounce of gold was worth $20.67. Every other currency was "pegged" to gold at some rate. These rates were not pulled out of thin air but were in line with what the bill of exchange market had set as a range.

If a country was spending more on stuff from another country than it could earn selling stuff to that country, one of two things had to happen under the gold standard. First, in the good case, the selling country could decide to use the money it earned to buy up assets in the deficit country. This is how things generally worked between Britain and the United States. The United States was always sucking in British investment for things like railways and factories priced in dollars. Britain was earning lots of dollars selling stuff like locomotives and machinery for the same railways and factories. This was pretty much a wash, most of the time. The bad case happened when the U.S. railways and factories got overbuilt and started to lose money. High finance stopped buying dollars. British exporters would then find fewer takers for the U.S. dollars they were earning and demand cash (gold) payment in London. The U.S. bankers would literally have to ship enough gold to London to cover the trade deficit at $20.67 per ounce.

The good news: The dollar would absolutely keep its value. The English sellers could count on turning gold into pounds at their own peg, so trade would continue smoothly. The bad news: Less gold reserves in the U.S. banks meant fewer dollars in paper money and bank deposits. In other words, fewer dollars would be available for U.S. businesses to borrow. This would always cause a slow down and could cause companies and banks to go bust suddenly. This would sometimes trigger a "panic" as businesses and banks rushed to be paid any cash they were owed. However, when the dust settled, wages would have fallen as jobs disappeared and so would prices. Fewer imports would be bought. So, domestic producers would enjoy lower costs. The country could export more and import less. Gold would return from abroad, and lending would increase. Better business conditions would restore company profits, and high finance would resume investing.

WINNERS AND LOSERS

So, did the gold standard really work? The real question is, for whom did it work? As an automatic adjustment, it protected the value of money. If you were a saver, even a small saver, the value of your nest egg was assured. If you were in high finance, you could put money to work anywhere on earth that offered you good returns. The same went for businesses and merchants involved in world trade. Overall, despite short, sharp shocks to countries living beyond their means, the rate of economic growth during the gold standard era was impressive.

However, if you were a worker or farmer, the whole weight of currency adjustment fell on you. The value of money was protected, but wages, employment, and prices were left to find their own level. Creditors—people who were owed money—were protected when debts retained their full value. Debtors often found themselves with less income to pay off loans they had taken out in good times. The trade it helped grow also made many people economic winners but others very vocal economic losers. The gold standard and free trade could be sustained through boom and bust in Britain and her empire only because it was governed by men who believed that property rights and commercial contracts were sacred and that the first duty of the government was to defend them. Most workers did not qualify as voters, let alone women and the poor. Most other countries were even less democratic in their domestic politics and felt free to follow Britain's example. America was the exception that proved the rule, a vast, rich country with a vibrant popular democracy (at least for white males) and a unique, often dysfunctional financial system.

DEMOCRACY AND SOUND MONEY

American democracy and sound money never did get along very well. Common human nature dictates that political democracy and individual property rights will always clash. If I owe somebody money, it is always easier for me to blame them than to pay them. There will always be politicians to tell me that I am a victim and that bankers are all villains to get my vote. Fear and loathing of financial power and the wealthy minority that controls it are easy to whip up, especially in hard times, as the recent AIG bonus hysteria amply demonstrates.

Finance Becomes National

Politicians and journalists outside the English speaking world, especially Europeans, are prone to rant against a system they call "Anglo-Saxon" capitalism and take smug satisfaction in its current crisis. In fact, there is no such system or ideology but rather the messy results of real history that made Britain and her colonial offspring, including the United States, rich and dynamic economies. Things would have turned out differently if Napoleon had succeeded or Lincoln had failed. However, Bagehot is right in insisting that confident use of credit and risk-taking in financial markets was a British habit shared by few other nations outside the English speaking world. Attachment to individual rights, especially property rights, limiting the power of government and the rule of law are all products of lucky historical accidents that allowed the English style of finance to triumph globally down to the present day. In this model, the financial markets themselves are the very center of the financial world, with banks, investment banks, and institutional investors orbiting around them somewhat randomly with little or no formal government control or direction.

EVERY BANK SYSTEM IS UNIQUE

Other nations with very different histories and cultures developed very different banking and financial systems. In almost every case, the state played a bigger role and markets a smaller one. Often these countries would try to copy the Bank of England, as France did in 1803, without understanding that what made it effective was the market it anchored. However, even more often, their own histories and cultures led them to develop different solutions altogether. The Dutch in particular adapted and spread the Italian public bank model (Bank of Amsterdam, 1609) for clearing and settling bills and payments. Over time, public banks and a payment clearing system called giro (named after the famous Banco di Giro in Venice) became central to the commercial and financial life of northern and eastern Europe. So did government-sponsored savings institutions at the local and national level. This model was later copied by Japan. Things that were central to English finance like checks, private banknotes, and debt and equity markets were far less prominent in these systems. The specifics for every country were a bit different based on different accidents of history including patterns of conquest and colonization.

The details don't matter. The key point is that while international high finance is a global ecology where all the creatures play by "Anglo-Saxon" rules, every country has its own unique banking, financial, and payment system serving it own economy and society. A bank account in Italy does not work precisely like a bank account in Germany, far less a British or American account. The same is true for investments, insurance, payment cards, and just about all the other financial stuff you and I use in our daily lives.

People are very conservative about things that involve money, for obvious reasons, so these varied national institutions are deeply entrenched and hard to change. They all have stood the test of time. They work for the people who use them. Some technology tweaks aside, nothing really new in banking and finance has been invented for centuries.

5

▼

THE FED DEMYSTIFIED

Once upon a time, perfectly sane adults believed in a Wizard who could make them rich and happy. His name was Alan Greenspan. He was small, and old, and spoke in a language nobody could quite understand. But he was a very great Wizard because everyone believed it was so. In fact, when asked what he would do if the great Wizard died, John McCain once suggested putting dark glasses on Greenspan and propping him up like the dead boss in the movie *Weekend at Bernie's.*

Throughout the long years when financial market excesses were slowly building into a volcanic eruption, the Wizard did two things that made us all happy and many of us rich. First, he managed to keep money and credit cheap and abundant. Second, he moved quickly to bail out financial markets every time they overplayed their hand. Market players came to believe in a "Greenspan put" that would always be available to them if things went south. Since they would suffer no pain if they fell, the acrobats of high finance felt free to swing higher and higher. They lost the wholesome fear of falling to earth. The Wizard had made their world risk free: Heads I win, tails the Fed will bail me out.

Today the Wizard is "in disgrace with fortune and men's eyes" and so is the whole magical circus he presided over. It now appears that cheap, abundant credit was the root of all evil, and the Wizard was the drug king-pin who supplied the pushers on Wall Street. Despite this, we retain a degree of faith in the Federal Reserve system itself that is downright touching. The new Wizard, Ben Bernanke, seems a kindly man. He has appeared in the flesh on *60 Minutes* to assure us all will be well, something the old Wizard would never do. We all want to believe that the "Fed" can save us, as it has in the past. However, our faith in the power and efficacy of the Fed or any other central bank to deliver economic salvation is largely based on a lack of understanding of what such creatures can and cannot do. As usual, we begin with a dose of "real history."

ORIGINS OF CENTRAL BANKING

In Chapter Three, we met government-chartered public banks, first in Italy, then in England. These were always privately owned, but they enjoyed government monopolies in return for managing its debt. They were mainly interested in making money for their shareholders. To maximize their profits, they used their unfair government privileges to compete with all other banks. They were resented by all the other bankers but were at times very useful.

The Bank of England in particular groped its way by trial and error towards something like today's central bank. The calculus was simple. The bank was the biggest player in the London money market and its directors were some of the largest merchants. Financial panics hit them hard in the wallet, so the bank used its deep pockets and government backing to stop them. This was pure self-interest; nothing in the bank's charter obliged it to do so. Indeed, this was a central theme in Bagehot's *Lombard Street*: How the bank had acted and should in the future act to stem market panics. His advice was simple: Since in a panic everybody wants to be paid immediately and nobody wants to lend at any price, the panic will end if and when it becomes clear that the bank will lend as much money as the market needs. This is something like what the Fed and other central banks attempted in 2008, but with a twist. Bagehot had two key conditions he wanted the bank to put on lending to prevent banks from getting into trouble over and over again.

First, the bank should lend to anyone with "good security"—meaning loans and securities with real value. Remember, the other banks were its rivals, so instead of playing favorites, the bank should only look at the quality of their assets. Second, the loans should be made at high "penal" rates. This helped restore confidence by drawing private money out of people's mattresses and from overseas and into the market where it was needed. Bank of England lending would be multiplied by private resources. The inflow of money from overseas would also prop up the value of the pound, another boost to confidence. As soon as banks began borrowing and lending between themselves, their use of high-cost Bank of England loans would fall off and the market would return to its normal, dull state. Meanwhile, the banks that had really screwed up would have not been able to show the bank enough good security. They would be allowed to go under and their business would go to better-run banks. The Bank of England did something very much like this in 1873, and it worked. J.P. Morgan acted the same way when he personally ended the panic of 1907 in New York by taking all the other bankers into his library one by one and making them come clean about their loans and investments. He decided which banks deserved loans and which needed to be merged or shut down. It worked, though the politicians in Washington never forgave him for saving the economy when they could not. The idea that a private, profit-maximizing banker could be the "lender of last resort" for the whole system drove them nuts. Despite nearly a century of populist resistance to a government-sponsored bank, Congress passed the Federal Reserve Act in 1913.

A CAMEL IS BORN

Like almost all legislative sausage-making in Congress, the Federal Reserve Act was an ugly compromise. Congress represented strong local interests in their states. Their constituents feared evil "Eastern Bankers" and, even more, evil foreign money men who lived to suck blood out of the working man and the farmer.

In this event, the Federal Reserve was born a camel, which is to say a horse designed by a committee. Instead of one central bank in the nation's financial capital, New York, Congress set up a system of twelve Federal Reserve Banks, some in places like Atlanta, Richmond, and Dallas that at the time had little national significance but very important senators. Each of these would act as the central bank of a region called a Reserve District. The Federal Reserve Bank of Boston was to be the reserve holder for the First District, the Federal Reserve Bank of San Francisco for the Twelfth District, and so on. The idea was that the deposit money of each community and region would be put to work providing credit for local businesses and farms. Each Reserve Bank had its own president and a board made up of bankers and business leaders in the district to ensure local control. On the top of the twelve regional Reserve Banks sat the Board of Governors of the Federal Reserve System. This was meant to be a coordinating body, not a central bank like the Bank of England. It was based in Washington, far from any financial center, and the regional bank presidents made up most of the board and key committees. However, The chairman and vice-chairman were presidential appointments confirmed by the Senate. As originally conceived, the Board of Governors had little power to set interest rates or the money supply nationally in this decentralized system. Nobody thought they were putting a wizard in charge of the economy.

How real history worked out was of course entirely different. Before the Fed was set up, almost all the extra OPM in America ended up concentrated in New York banks. This was inevitable because Wall Street had become the financial capital of the country well before the Civil War, and money attracts money. Without a central bank, the United States had improvised a system of banking based on "fractional reserves." Simply put, the thousands of small-town banks across America kept their cash reserves in larger "reserve city" banks. The so-called reserve cities were commercial hubs like Chicago or Cleveland. It was expected that these banks would lend to their country cousins as needed, but stock trading and high finance were concentrated in New York. The reserve city banks kept their own reserve and the money placed with them by country banks in New York because they got much better returns. So a small-town dentist in Iowa ended up funding Wall Street stock speculators. When Wall Street crashed, as it did in 1907, the reserves kept in New York banks were frozen or disappeared. Small-town banks couldn't borrow or get their own funds back, businesses and farmers couldn't get credit, and Main Street went bust. This was exactly what Congress wanted to stop by setting up the Fed.

THE BEAST IS TAMED

The New York banks, led by J.P. Morgan himself, liked having most of the country's banking reserve in their vaults. Yet they eventually threw their support behind The Federal Reserve Act as it moved through Congress. They did this for two reasons. First, they knew Washington couldn't really make the Fed work without them, and as long as they could control the Federal Reserve Bank of New York, things would not really change much. Second, the United States simply didn't have a workable payments system.

Sure, the government-issued coinage and greenbacks were legal tender, but the banks made no money on them and they were not suited for large transactions. Big U.S. companies had always drawn bills of exchange on London banks, but domestic bill use was limited.

That left checks. The United States was awash in checks ever since the greenback became the federal paper currency in 1862 and quickly pushed banks out of the note-issuing business. Checks, however, worked poorly outside the local area in which they were written. With tens of thousands of small banks, only the big-city banks who held their reserves could take the risk of clearing them. They always held something back, so checks could not be collected "at par," meaning for their face value. Therefore, a $1000 in New York could be collected for $1000 in the New York Clearing House, but a $1000 check from Birmingham or Oakland might only fetch $900 after all the banks it passed through had given it a haircut. A check could pass from a country bank in California, to Oakland, to San Francisco, to Chicago, and eventually to New York, losing value every step of the way. This was manna from heaven for all the "through" banks but a pain in the neck for national companies like U.S. Steel and their bankers like J.P. Morgan. As the railway tied America together into a single national economy, a workable check clearing system became a priority for men like Morgan. He got the bankers to back the Federal Reserve scheme because it mandated that checks be paid at their face value.

Morgan also got his man, Ben Strong, as the first president of the Federal Reserve Bank of New York. This was at the time, and remains so now, the only part of the system that really can act like a central bank. Wall Street was the only thing in America remotely comparable with the great London loan pool. Not only the stock market, but markets in bonds issued by corporations and both the Federal government and the states were all concentrated there. So were the deposits of the banking system, despite the intentions of Congress. The Federal Reserve System, in fact, made the movement of money to New York easier. Regional banks might keep their reserve at Fed accounts in other districts but could transfer extra money to the accounts of banks in the New York Fed. From 1918 onwards, the Federal Reserve offered a telegraphic transfer system that did this within a day for member banks.

The big New York banks, led by Morgan, started a telephone market in what is still called "Fed Funds." Using their extensive contacts in smaller banks across the country, the New York banks could bid for excess reserves to borrow overnight. Many of these short-term loans went to fund the positions of stock traders on Wall Street. The U.S. banking system remained as exposed to the ups and downs of Wall Street as ever.

This was unavoidable. Money as we said always seeks money. Before the First World War, the United States had modest government debt and New York had never developed anything like the huge market in bills and bankers acceptances that fed the London money market. Much riskier corporate equities and bonds were Wall Street's stock in trade. Congress had willed a central bank into existence, but nobody including Ben Strong really knew how to make one work properly.

A LITTLE HELP FROM MY FRIENDS

Ben Strong and the New York Fed became great friends with the Bank of England. This included a strong personal bond with Montagu Norman, the long-serving (1920–1944) governor of the bank. World War I had ended London's global financial supremacy, so Norman's mission was to see that New York, the new top dog, was properly trained. Norman was old school and wanted to get the world back on the gold standard that had been suspended during the war. Strong agreed, and bent his efforts on preserving the value of the dollar relative to gold. This meant keeping the supply of money in check. The Bank of England could do this through its money market operations. The New York Fed learned to manage the amount of money in the banking system through so-called open market operations. The war had created a big market in U.S. treasury bonds. Banks were the biggest holders of the bonds. By selling bonds it held at attractive prices, the Fed could drain excess cash from the banks, raising rates by reducing the supply of credit. By going into the market to buy up bonds, the Fed could add cash to the system and push down rates. This wasn't built into the design of the Federal Reserve System. The New York Fed learned to play the open market game with a little help from its friends in London.

THE DISCOUNT WINDOW

In fact, the tool envisioned for the twelve Federal Reserve Banks in the legislation was the old Bank of England standby of the discount window. This is a real place in the Bank of England building where banks and bill brokers bring financial paper acceptable to the bank to borrow cash. In London, this was a normal operation—the Bank of England was, after all, a privately owned bank that needed to make a living lending money. Its discount rate was the key rate because it was the biggest player. In America, banks were shy about being seen at the discount window, even though each of the new buildings built for the twelve district banks had a discrete discount window modeled on that of the Bank of England. The thousands of local banks in America and their big-city cousins had a long history of borrowing and lending among themselves before the Fed was set up. Going to the discount window at the Fed implied that a bank was in trouble and couldn't borrow from its peers. Therefore, banks avoided using the Fed as it was intended to be used, as a supplier of credit to its member banks. The discount rate was and remains the one rate of interest the Fed can set on its own. It is also among the least important.

FED FUNDS

If and when you read or listen to financial news, the so-called Fed Funds rate is mentioned all the time, especially after the Board of Governors meet in Washington. We are told the Fed has cut the Fed Funds rate or has raised the Fed Funds rate as a result of discussions at that meeting. This is the Great Oz in action, moving markets around the world. It is also nonsense, pure and simple. Fed Funds is shorthand for the overnight market in which banks with extra money in the Federal Reserve accounts rent that money to banks that are short. The Fed Funds rate isn't set by the Fed in a mechanical way. It is a market rate that goes up and down with the supply of short-term cash in the banking system. The Fed Funds rate is simply a target rate the Fed hopes to achieve through its open-market operations. The real work is done by the bond traders at the New York Fed open market desk. The key point is that the Fed works through the market. Its power to do anything directly is limited to a couple of levers, mainly setting reserve policy (required levels, what interest, if any, to pay banks) and rules for its discount window (who can borrow, and on what terms).

THE FED'S FIRST BIG TEST

During the 1920s, Ben Strong's New York Fed joined the big boys club of central banks, including the Bank of England, the Bank of France, and the German Reichsbank. The Fed had no pedigree, but America had all the money after the war. The European Allies owed the American's big time for war loans, and the Germans owed the Allies big time for war damages, but claimed they couldn't pay. So everything depended on an America deeply resentful of being suckered into the war in the first place. Without going into detail, the war debt problem was eventually finessed, largely through setting up a central banker's bank in Switzerland called the Bank of International Settlement (BIS). The BIS remains a global club for central bankers, a Hogwarts for financial wizards. What all the wizards could agree on was that central bankers were very clever and serious men who understood things that mere mortals, especially elected politicians, couldn't begin to fathom.

The central belief of the wizards was that the first responsibility of a central bank was to maintain sound money. To the wizards, this meant the gold standard needed to be restored—all countries had suspended payments in gold during the war—and defended. This was sound Victorian economic orthodoxy. The problem was that it had been designed for a global financial system centered on London's strong banks and deep money market. These had been much reduced by the War. The United States had money but relatively puny banks—Morgan an exception—and a frothy stock market.

Very much like the run-up to the 2008 crisis, the 1920s saw a U.S. stock market mania of epic proportions based on new technologies like radio and the automobile. Paper fortunes in the stock market in turn fueled real estate and consumption booms. Wages did not keep pace, and farm prices actually fell. Nobody seemed to care, except Ben Strong. He thought that too much stock market speculation was happening, mostly financed on loose credit. Farmers were failing, and small town banks were collapsing at an alarming rate as money was sucked into New York. The Fed moved to deflate the bubble by reigning in the money supply sharply.

THE GREAT DEPRESSION

We are doomed to debate the causes and course of the Great Depression forever. You can't turn on a news or money show where the events of 2008 are not compared with the 1930s. Everyone, from left to right, draws the lessons they want. What is clear is that in October of 1929 stock market prices crashed after the Fed began trying to reign in credit. This need not, in and of itself, cause a panic. Bubbles can deflate without bursting. What is less clear and highly important to you and me today is, why did a stock market panic, a pretty normal occurrence in New York, turn into a global depression? The stock answer to this question, especially among Democrats, has been to blame it all on the policies of Herbert Hoover, the George Bush of his day. This is political slander, although it proved an effective one for generations. The real culprit in the eyes of many historians was the Federal Reserve.

Basically, Ben Strong applied the Bagehot formula badly. The essential thing in a panic is to assure the market that the central bank will meet all legitimate demands for credit, though on tough terms. The key concept is to lend freely and quickly as much money as is required to halt the panic. The notion of only lending on good security was meant to weed out the reckless banks that had become insolvent.

That was fine for Victorian London. In real-life America, the credit bubble of the 1920s, like that from 1998 to 2008, left the leading banks stuffed with rotten loans and with no good security to borrow against, at any price. Today, the rotten securities are mostly securitized assets based on mortgages and other consumer loans. Back then, the real problem was that banks had directly (or indirectly through stock brokers) loaned people too much money to buy stocks on "margin." A margin loan allows you to buy a share of stock with the broker's money paying for most of it. During the bull market of the twenties, it was possible to buy $1000 of stock for ten or twenty dollars. When stocks keep going up, this is a great way to turn a little money into a lot of money.

If stocks plunge, the borrower is asked to put up more "margin," cash to cover the difference between the loan and the value of the stock. If customers can meet these margin calls, fine. If they can't, banks could find themselves with a $1000 loan the borrower cannot possibly pay by selling stock. Borrowers walk away, leaving the bank with trash stocks. With their paper wealth wiped out, these same borrowers began defaulting on mortgages and other loans. Banks began to call in loans to raise cash, sending more customers into the tank. Soon, banks began to fail in large numbers, triggering more bank runs.

Between the end of 1920 and FDR's famous Bank Holiday of 1933, about 5,000 of America's roughly 30,000 banks failed. Essentially, Ben Strong and the Federal Reserve Board let them fail, judging it irresponsible to bail out banks that made themselves insolvent. However, in banking, timing is everything. There is a very thin line between insolvency—being basically unable to pay your debts for lack of income or assets—and illiquidity—being unable to pay now because you can't get the cash. Bagehot viewed a panic in the money market as a liquidity problem for everybody, whether they are solvent or insolvent—no one in this situation will lend. The Bank of England or any central bank can solve a liquidity crisis by lending quickly and freely until the fear dies down. There will be plenty of opportunities to bury the insolvent later. If a panic is a fire, money is a hose. The first order of business is to beat down the flames.

This is precisely what the Federal Reserve failed to do in 1930. It kept money too tight, failed to bail out the banks, and in the process dried up money and credit in the real economy. Businesses closed, employment collapsed, more businesses closed, and so forth in a downward spiral. Until 2009, it seemed impossible that the world would be capable of repeating the tragedy of the 1930s. The philosopher George Santayana famously said that "Those who forget history are destined to repeat it," but he failed to warn us that you can remember history and still end up repeating it.

HELICOPTER BEN

Ben Strong, to be fair, had no guidance about how to be a central banker aside from what his friend Montagu told him. Ben Bernanke, our current wizard, has spent his academic career trying to understand what went wrong in the 1930s. His conclusion is that the Fed should have thrown open the floodgates and created as much money and credit as possible. He even once spoke about dropping bales of money from helicopters if need be. This earned him the nickname Helicopter Ben, which in part accounts for the generally good reception the market gave him when he succeeded Alan Greenspan as Board Chairman. The markets had always counted on the Greenspan put and Bernanke seemed likely to throw money at problems too. During 2008 and 2009, the Fed became very aggressive about taking loans onto its own balance sheet, expanding which firms could qualify for the discount window (if you are not yet a bank holding company, you can probably sign up using Legal Zoom) and cutting rates to the bone.

The problem might just have been that the Fed did not act quickly and radically enough given the scale and speed of the market implosion. But perhaps this is unfair. It is hard to be ahead of the curve in a tsunami. However, the Old Lady of Threadneedle Street—as the Bank of England used to be known—has been faster to act in the current situation and has in many ways been more radical. Helicopter Ben might have been well advised to take his cues from Governor King as much as Ben Strong took his from Montagu. Only time will tell, but Bagehot surely would have supported a bold, consistent policy over scrambling from weekend bank rescue to weekend bank rescue on a case-by-case, seat-of-your-pants basis. These are ad hoc rescues, and the constant changing of the rules has more or less convinced banks and investors that they cannot trust the Federal government to set rules and play by them.

TO THE LAST BULLET

On January 22, 1879, a British column of nearly 2,000 soldiers equipped with Martini-Henry rifles and cannon was overrun and massacred by 20,000 Zulu warriors in a battle that made Custer's last stand look like a tea party. Modern study of the battlefield in South Africa confirms that the British were destroyed because, despite a more than ample supply of bullets, their supply sergeant did not get them up to the firing line fast enough. When their fire slackened, the Zulu warriors quickly overran the firing line, killing every last man in it. The British got the pace of the battle wrong. They were trained to prevail in a sustained fight. The Zulus were quick and bold and had the discipline to use their advantage in numbers. The only chance to beat them was to pour overwhelming fire into them early in the fight. Conserving ammunition was fatal.

In 2009, the Fed and other central banks began running out of bullets. They might well have done better using the bullets they did have much sooner. Remember, the basic thing that a central bank can do is to either increase or decrease interest rates through injecting or draining money from the banks. All things being equal, lower rates encourage more borrowing. Higher rates discourage borrowing. Borrowing costs influence business activity and the price of stuff, so central banks raise rates when the economy becomes overheated and cut them when it becomes sluggish. But when you cannot cut rates because they're at zero and the economy is still in the tank, your powers as a wizard begin to fail. Low rates only work if businesses have the confidence to borrow and hire people who will spend. They are not a substitute for confidence. This is where we find ourselves today. And we have company. Japan was in the same pickle for much of the 1990s.

DEFLATION

The real nightmare is something called deflation. You and I have lived our whole lives in the shadow of inflation. The purchasing power of money always seems to erode. However, the train can run in the opposite direction. Prices can, and over long periods of time have, fallen. A dollar in 1900 bought a lot more than a dollar in 1800 because the world had become a lot better at making and transporting stuff. You also get a lot more PC function and memory for each dollar you spend than you got five or ten years ago. Spread over time or in specific products, price deflation can be good for living standards. Sudden deflation is a different story. After the bursting of the Japanese

bubble economy of the 1980s, real estate values tumbled 80% or 90% overnight, and the stock market gave up all its gains. Something similar happened in 1930s America. Houses that cost tens of thousands to build fetched a few hundred at sheriff's auctions. Car sales fell through the floor, driving down the prices of all models. Even people who remained solidly employed did not spend their money because they thought things would be cheaper tomorrow.

On the other hand, the more the price of stuff falls, the more the value of money increases. Consciously or not, you and I are used to the idea of borrowing a quarter million dollars today to buy a house with a thirty-year mortgage because we know the house will probably be worth a million at the end of the loan. Our total borrowing cost will only be about half that, and each of those dollars will be worth less in the future than today. In a world of deflation, the house might be worth only $100,000 in thirty years, but our borrowing cost will be around five times that amount, with each dollar being worth more than it is today. Only a chump will borrow when expecting deflation, just as only a chump will spend in the same conditions.

The simple fact of the matter is that nobody really knows how to get out of this kind of deflationary spiral once it gains momentum. The idea that the usual shot of cheap money won't work puts real terror into central bankers and their political masters. This explains the sudden revival of the ideas and reputation of John Maynard Keynes.

THE GHOST OF LORD KEYNES

Keynes was never what the press or politicians would call a Keynesian. He was pragmatic for an intellectual and made a small fortune speculating in stocks. His famous book, which nobody reads, *The General Theory*, was largely concerned with solving the problem posed by deflation. This is called the "paradox of thrift" or the "liquidity trap." If you stop spending money because your job is uncertain and things are getting cheaper all the time, you are doing the right thing for you. But if everyone does this, spending and work dry up and you have a deflationary spiral leading to a prolonged depression like that of the 1930s.

Keynes' solution to deflation was based on the idea that the economy was driven by total demand for goods and services. In fact, he more or less invented the national accounts we use to measure GNP, or Gross National Product, another term everyone hears in the news without really understanding what it means. What it really measures is what consumers, businesses, and governments spend and invest. The more spending, the better for employment and growth, at least until demand for goods drives up prices too fast. In a slump, all that matters is jacking up total demand to get folks back to work. If business and consumers don't spend enough, the government will have to take up the slack by increasing its spending and borrowing. It doesn't matter what government spends money on—Keynes thought it was better to pay people to dig holes and fill them up than to leave them without jobs and income. And Keynes certainly didn't advocate permanent big-government spending programs. He was trying to get the world out of a hole that nobody knew how to get out of. Governments could cut back their spending when normal consumers and business demand was restored. It took Keynes' American followers to turn his ideas into today's liberal orthodoxy.

WORLD WAR AS STIMULUS

In the event, Keynes' *General Theory* was quickly overtaken by the outbreak of general war in Europe and Asia in 1939. It has been truly, if shockingly, said that "war is health of the state." Raising armies and building fleets are some of the few things governments can do effectively. In the process, this generates incredible demands for labor and materials. Before any of Keynes' ideas were tried, the Depression had ended in the process of defeating Hitler's New Order, not through Roosevelt's New Deal program. War is not only an overwhelming government "stimulus" program, it also always ends. Social spending— or "investments" in Washington-new speak—are terrible stimulus programs because they are almost impossible to cut back or even contain once voters come to depend on them. World War II not only got America out of the Depression, but much of the demand it generated was replaced by more wholesome consumer and business spending as the invasion of Normandy was succeeded by the invasion of Levittown and the Baby Boom.

Even if Keynes' ideas were never properly tried, his reputation and influence allowed him to dominate the single most important economic conference of all time.

A WORLD RESTORED: THE DOLLAR BECOMES THE NEW GOLD

The Conference held at the Bretton Woods Hotel in New Hampshire during 1944 was a blend of British brain and American brawn acting to put the world economy back together. Keynes had the plan, and the United States had the money.

The big idea was to turn the U.S. dollar into the global reserve currency, meaning the money that all central banks paid each other in to settle the "balance of payments" mismatches that always arose from cross-border trade and investment. Under the old gold standard, the global reserve currency was the British Pound but only because it was fully convertible to gold at a fixed rate. The new Bretton Woods system pegged each country's currency to the U.S. dollar within a fixed range and in turn pegged the dollar to gold. A machinery called the International Monetary Fund (IMF) was set up to police the whole system and provide dollar loans to countries having temporary balance of payments problems. The United States was the biggest shareholder in the IMF and provided the largest chunk of its resources. A sister organization called the World Bank was set up alongside the IMF to provide low-cost loans and technical assistance to poor countries. Again, the United States was a major stakeholder. As the European empires dissolved after the war, scores of new nation states were formed. Each established a central bank, and most of them became clients of the two Washington-based organizations just described.

REVIVING TRADE

A third key organization set up at the end of the war was the General Agreement of Tariffs and Trade, a sort of floating international conference that eventually morphed into the World Trade Organization. Keynes and his colleagues understood the big role the collapse in trade between countries had played in deepening and prolonging the Great Depression and setting the world on the road to war. Again, this was an organization dependent on American leadership.

This international financial architecture worked remarkably well as long as it suited U.S. interests and did not attract too much attention from Congress. The post-war recovery of global trade and investment flows that restored growth to the developed economies of the world would have been difficult if not impossible without it.

THE PROBLEMS OF U.S. POLITICS

The great vulnerability of the system was that it ultimately rested on the whims of American domestic politics. These were very different than British politics where the importance of trade and finance to the country was widely understood. Most Americans were unconcerned with the global economy and had no understanding of how it benefited them. Congress reflected this, and so at times did American presidents. America has always found it harder to do the right thing in international economic policy but has risen to the challenge at critical moments with remarkable frequency. Think of the Marshall Plan.

THE LENDER OF LAST RESORT TO THE WORLD

The key point from the point of view of understanding the current crisis is that the United States had in the post-war world become, willy nilly, the "lender of last resort" in an increasingly connected financial system that revolved around the dollar. When countries like Mexico or Argentina fell into financial crises, the United States was the only country that could stave off collapse. The IMF was really a beard behind which U.S. taxpayer money could be used to bail out the world economy when crises got bad enough to threaten American interests. It made the American role less visible to both the country being saved and, most importantly, to the U.S. public.

What the system never envisioned was that the U.S. financial system itself would be the source of a crisis that infected all of the other financial systems of the world

6

▼

The Limits of Financial Regulation

It is a common and perverse myth of partisan politics that it was the financial deregulation—something that gained momentum in the United States during the 1980s and 1990s and was largely complete before the Bush years—that led directly to the 2008 crisis. A more accurate depiction of things is that deregulation, like regulation, is a trailing rather than a causal factor. Deregulation, such as it was, largely occurred because the U.S. financial system was already in the midst of a jailbreak. The New Deal regulatory prison walls had been breached by global capital markets and technology.

Money, as we have seen, is a kind of fluid that greases buying and selling, based on saving and borrowing. Like water, it seeks its own level and breaks down dams or goes over and around them. As we saw in Chapter Four, the U.S. financial system was woefully underdeveloped for an advanced economy before the 1929 crash. The New Deal preserved its worst aspects, especially weak local banks, added new complexity, regulated the whole thing to an absurd extent, and made it hostage to partisan politics. No other country outside the communist bloc, not even socialist France or Sweden, has tried so comprehensively to tame markets and protect the "little guy" from financial risk.

RULES OF THE GAME

During the recent election campaign, you were told endlessly that the financial crisis was the result of the lack of an obviously good thing called "regulation." If a politician says something emphatically and repeats it endlessly, the chances are pretty good that it is a lie. Regulation means, literally, rules making. There are many reasons to make rules for any voluntary organization. My club in London has lots of them, and a committee to enforce them. Nobody forced me to join. The rules simply codify common sense and mutual courtesy. They make life better for the members. Every sport has developed a set of rules and people to interpret and enforce its rules during play called referees, literally those who you refer to for a ruling. These rules were developed over time by actual players and associations of players to make fair competition possible. By observing the known rules and etiquette of golf, any two people who know the game can have a fair match anywhere on earth. The same is true of basketball, tennis, rugby, football, soccer, or even chess and bridge.

What club rules and game rules do not pretend to do is make things "fair" in the way that many politicians use the word. A club selects its own members on an arbitrary basis. Nobody has a right to join or grounds to complain of exclusion, though the modern cult of equality would dispute this. Rules of a game do not confer equal rights to win to the competitors. Skill, talent, practice, and luck determine outcomes, and these are very unevenly distributed. Outcomes are equally lopsided. One doesn't play golf with Tiger Woods expecting to beat him. You only have a right to expect that he is observing the rules of the game.

BEWARE THE RULE MAKER

Now imagine what would happen if, in the interest of making life fair, rules were imposed by lawyers and bureaucrats on popular games. They would be acting under laws passed by politicians seeking the votes of people lacking the skill, talent, and dumb luck to win at games they wanted to play. Almost everybody writing the laws and rules or involved in enforcing them would be totally ignorant of the traditional rules of the game. In fact, they wouldn't know how it was really played. They would take pride in this ignorance, believing a better game could be devised using legislative and legal sanctions, including fines and imprisonment, to protect losers from winners. For example, they could regulate excessive height in basketball. Of course, the sheer absurdity of such a project would stop it in its tracks.

However, politicians and lawyers with no functioning comprehension of how finance and the market economy work—listen to any congressional hearing or presidential news conference to confirm this—find it appropriate to call for more regulation of these activities. These days most of us are inclined to listen to them. In doing so, we put our future prosperity and freedom at risk.

THE RULE OF LAW

Real history shows two things that we should take into account. First, the rule of law is essential to the functioning of any market, but regulation as such is not. Second, the most highly regulated markets and institutions are just as liable to blow up as unregulated ones, indeed even more so. This book has spent a lot of time in Walter Bagehot's London simply because so much of modern finance was born there. The shocking fact is that until quite recently, formal regulation was largely absent in the London financial markets, which were conducted by self-regulating clubs under the watchful eyes of the Bank of England. There was not even a general law defining banking until 1979. What London did have was the common law, including age-old concepts like fraud, theft, and neglect of fiduciary duty. The law was also a firm upholder of the sanctity of property rights and the enforcement of contracts. The law courts of England, especially those with jurisdiction over the City of London, relied on something called the "law merchant," where respected participants in a market could advise the court what fair customary practice was and was not. In other words, what rules the game was played by were set according to the players. The role of statute law was very limited. For example, the famous Bill of Exchange Act of 1882 and subsequent amendments of it came about because so many cases concerning the rights and obligations of holders of bills and checks had come into the courts. The act just cleaned up and codified what the courts had been deciding for generations. Various acts of Parliament also chartered the Bank of England and modified its privileges and monopolies over time, but outside of these markers, literally anyone could enter the business of banking. Legally, a bank was simply a business recognized as a bank by other bankers, just as a stock broker was a member of the stock exchange, a private club free to select its own members.

COMMERCIAL HONOR

The City of London was only a mile square, and mostly everyone knew each other personally or by reputation. There was no place to start over if you screwed up. There were no second chances. The old notion that a gentleman's word was his bond—in other words as good as his signed contract—grew up in London not because people were better or more honest there, but because not playing by the rules had a big downside. Of course, "fair" within the clubby confines of London would be very "unfair" to an American (or even a British) politician of today. The various clubs looked after their own. For example, the banks all colluded to an extent to keep the interest rates they charged customers from being driven down by competition. Insider trading—that is, taking advantage of inside dope to beat the market—was perfectly OK among stock brokers. In fact, there was little pretense that the interest of outsiders like you and me were equal to those of the club members. Outright frauds and cheats were bad for business, though, and, aside from the penalties of law, being shunned by the key clubs and the Bank of England was the ultimate sanction.

IN THE LIFE BOAT

One of the prices of membership was pitching in to save the City of London when a crisis did arise. As head of the club—in fact if not in law—the Bank of England could more or less compel banks to bail out other banks if their failure was seen as a threat to the market. For example, in the 1970s, a group of so-called fringe or secondary banks sprang up that were financing property deals and writing second mortgages. When property prices collapsed, the Bank of England organized a "life boat" in which all the clearing house banks took part. The "lifeboat" succeeded in an orderly run off of the secondary banks' business, protecting their depositors and public confidence in banking. Banking history is full of instances when members of a clearing house save the system in a crisis. Something like this happened on more than one occasion in the New York Clearing House, for example, when the Civil War broke out and triggered a panic. In fact, no private clearing house has ever failed completely in a crisis.

The point is that while the rule of law is essential, formal regulation is not required for a robust and safe financial system. A clearing house can, as we saw in Chapter Four, impose standards on both its members and their own customers through naked self-interest. When big money is at stake, nobody does business with people they believe will cost them money by not doing what they promised to do. A clearing house is, at times of crisis, more like an incident of mutual hostage-taking than a club. All the members are distrustful rivals, but nobody gets paid unless everyone gets paid, so burdens and losses end up being shared. Leadership helps, but a privately owned Bank of England did as well at leading the bankers' clubs as did a government owned Bank of England. Lots of New York bankers hated J.P. Morgan, but they all took his lead in 1907.

THE CASE FOR FREE BANKING

There is good evidence in both real history and economic thought for the value of something called "free banking." This is not free checking. Rather, it is a theory that argues that the involvement of government in money and banking is almost always a bad thing. Up until the formation of the Bank of England, almost all banking was in fact "free," in England and most other countries. Anyone with the cash to discount bills of exchange for traders and was trusted to hold funds could be a banker. Every market town in Europe and the countries that Europe traded with had such bankers. Some thrived for generations and some went bust. Essentially, their customers took their chances and were sometimes proved wrong in that trust. We only replaced this system over the last century or so.

In looking at our 401(k) statements and at the nightly news, can we say our current financial system is that much better? Could "free banking" have done much worse? Bagehot used "real" history to demonstrate that the Bank of England and the whole shape of the London market was not a natural development but just an accident of seventeenth century politics. The countries who copied Britain and the establishment of the Bank of England confused effect—a big, robust financial market—with its cause. The Bank of England didn't so much create the vibrant London market as the London market made its success possible, and that success in turn influenced how the market evolved in both good and bad ways.

AMERICA AS THE HOME OF FREE BANKING

The U.S. experience shows that a country could thrive on something very close to free banking. Men like Hamilton and his wealthy Federalist friends tried to copy the Bank of England themselves at both the national and state level. Banks of the United States were in fact chartered by Congress in 1791 and in 1816. Democratic (with a small d) politics crushed the Bank of the United States twice, most famously under Andrew Jackson, who turned the destruction of the Second Bank of the United States into a personal vendetta. He believed he was defending democracy and the common man. Americans at the state level used to make it very easy to start banks because they so mistrusted concentrated financial power. We did little to supervise banks once chartered, except to restrict when they could do business—again so they could not grow large. The bottom line is that nineteenth-century America was a country in which governments made it easy for more or less anyone with some money and a few connections to start a bank. The result? One of the fastest rates of economic growth in history, powered by plentiful bank credit. Sure, as we noted previously, American banking was prone to bank runs and failures. Widows and orphans did get wiped out. However, American banking without a central bank or formal bank regulation worked very well in the more commercially developed regions like New England and in big cities generally. For example, New England bankers kept their reserves in a "bankers bank" called the Suffolk County Bank in Boston. In return, their notes and checks were always honored at par,

100 cents on the dollar. This voluntary private arrangement achieved what the Federal Reserve system did generations later.

Even today, with the largest banks crippled by so-called toxic assets and government meddling, free banking could restore credit to you and me by letting clean, "greenfield" banks be started by anyone with money to lend. In the U.K., Tesco, that country's equivalent of Wal-Mart, is going into full-service retail banking. Why not Wal-Mart and other big chains in the United States doing the same? The basic functions of a bank are not hard to perform. As Bagehot insisted, banking is as simple a business as can be conceived. It is mostly a matter of keeping books and knowing your customers. In the sudden absence of formal banks, a version of "free banking" always springs up. In the early 1970s, the Irish banking system—the Central Bank and the four check-clearing banks—was shut down by a strike that lasted months. Quinsworth, a supermarket chain, quickly emerged as a place people could cash checks and get credit. Life went on. Paddy Quinn had people's trust and knew his customers, so he, in effect, was a banker until the "real" banks reopened their doors.

GOVERNMENT AND THE ECONOMY

So if "free banking" is something that has been shown to work at many times and places, why is it never openly discussed outside of libertarian circles? The answer is that the formal banking system we know of today is a creature of government, pure and simple. This is not the result of any deep, dark conspiracy by closet communist. It is simply another accident of history.

Put simply, in the twentieth century, the power of government over its citizens has expanded as never before. We have ceased to be grown-ups. A free banking and financial system requires all of us to be grown-up and take full responsibility for our actions. This means that we should only put money in a bank we trusted. In Bagehot's day, London private banks never disclosed their financial condition to customers. The idea is, if you need a bank to prove it is trustworthy, you shouldn't put your money in it. Remember, finance is all a matter of faith. The downside, of course, is that if you are wrong, you can't expect to be bailed out. Beyond what you can recover through the courts, you eat your losses. The same should be true of investment or insurance policies—if you don't trust the seller, don't buy it. Roman law summed up this idea as *caveat emptor*, buyer beware. Free banking and free markets demand the freedom to fail, for banks and for companies and for you and me.

Not so long ago, say 1909, almost everyone in the English speaking world accepted this. Nobody in America or Britain thought that government was or could be responsible for managing the economy in a free country. Government management of the economy was the mark of less free countries like France, Germany, or Imperial Russia, where government bureaucrats were thick as fleas. Governments in the United States and United Kingdom were tiny by comparison and didn't even keep economic statistics—the word "unemployment" didn't even exist back then. Direct taxation of income was clearly unconstitutional in the United States until the 16th Amendment was passed in 1913, the same year the Federal Reserve Act became law.

THE BIRTH OF BIG GOVERNMENT

Suddenly, the government was getting the tools, at least in embryo, to manage and regulate the economy—something the Founding Fathers never could have imagined. How did this happen?

Three decisive changes explain a lot. First, economic power in America became radically concentrated by the rise of giant corporations like U.S. Steel and Standard Oil. This power was widely abused through monopoly and financial manipulation, producing an unlovable class of super-rich, vulgar plutocrats the press labeled as "robber barons," though to their credit most robber barons actually founded their companies, indeed whole industries, and many started life poor.

Second, the United States became an urban, industrial society where most people for the first time depended on formal employment in big companies for a living. Up until 1880 or so, most Americans more or less worked for themselves. By the early 1900s, the vast majority were "employees." They felt powerless and exploited, even though U.S. wages were in fact high by world standards. Mass immigration of Europe's poor added to both the reality and the visibility of misery in the midst of plenty. Immigrants also brought the radical politics of Europe, where industrialization had brought trade unionism, socialism, communism, and anarchism to the working class.

Third, starting in the states but reaching the White House in the person of Teddy Roosevelt, a progressive movement took root in American politics that stood traditional roles of government and the private economy on their head. America and Victorian Britain had been built upon a creed of protecting the liberty of the individual from the state that came to be called liberalism. The whole purpose of the Constitution was to prevent an active and overpowering government from smothering private rights and property. The progressives saw the opposite problem, the vast unaccountable power of big business smothering the little people's ability to lead a decent life. Teddy Roosevelt referred to the "malefactors of great wealth" who ran big business, and he saw it as the government's duty to take the side of the people against them. The idea that private power was more dangerous than the state took root, despite the clear lessons of history. The federal regulatory state that we all take as normal started out addressing clear threats to public health and safety like tainted food and dangerous drugs. Greedy businesses always provide enough scandals to allow the press to whip up a case for the government to act once the principle that economic regulation is legitimate takes hold. The problem is that once that principle is accepted as a general rule, it is hard to say what government *shouldn't* regulate in the name of the people.

THE PITY OF WAR

That question was soon answered by the First World War. The answer was: Government should regulate everything. With so-called war socialism in the Kaiser's Germany as an unspoken model, Britain and the United States regulated wages, prices, interest rates, transportation—the whole shooting match. Foreign exchange controls were slapped on, trade embargoed, and the gold standard was suspended. This was the only way to mobilize the resources required to fight a "total war" involving tens of million of combatants. It was full of absurdities and glitches, but it was tolerable for a few years. Above all, it was seen to be fair. Luxuries disappeared and necessities were rationed. All able-bodied men were drafted into military service. Death was democratic: Teddy Roosevelt and banker George Baker both lost aviator sons in France. The British upper classes were bled white. After 1920, the United States and United Kingdom tried to restore the pre-war order, including the gold standard. To a large degree they succeeded in restoring a measure of economic freedom, and the stock market boom of the Roaring Twenties seemed to justify this. However, the experience of total if temporary government control over the economy stuck with many. And, with the Bolshevik takeover of Russia in 1920, there was a living example of a great state run by government experts for the common good, without private wealth or markets. Western artists and intellectuals fell in love with the idea. The crash of 1929, the Depression, and the Second World War all pointed to the failure of free market capitalism. The state had a need and right to control the "commanding heights" of the economy, including banking and finance. By 1950, two-thirds of mankind lived under a Marxist command economy or a milder form of socialism that allowed for the inmates of the welfare state to vote for higher taxes and more social spending on themselves.

AMERICA THE EXCEPTION

America, despite the sometimes radical anti-business policies of the New Deal and an almost permanent Democratic congressional ascendancy from 1932 until 1994, remained a hold-out. In fact, Franklin Roosevelt himself was a pragmatic power player who reacted to events by trying new things. He was anything but a socialist, more a wealthy Hudson Valley squire with a mix of good intentions and ambition. In Europe or Japan, government bureaucrats often assumed direct control over how banks and market participants directed their lending. Often, major banks or whole banking systems were taken into state ownership. In America, we got our own peculiar solution: A private, profit-seeking financial system joined at the hip with a sprawling, contradictory, and highly political "regulatory state."

As we noted earlier, markets have always needed a rule of law. And they have always needed something the Bank of England used to call "supervision." This is not regulation, but more like having a grown-up supervise the playground so nobody gets hurt. In the United States, we have neither clear and certain law nor supervision by grown-ups. Instead, we have lawyers, thousands upon thousands of them, writing rules and regulations. Few if any of them know how banking and markets really work. They know how the laws and regulations work, which is how they cash in at banks and law firms after their stint in government service. Their value consists entirely in figuring out how to find ways to get around regulations.

THE REGULATORY STATE

The regulatory state lives in the bubble of Washington DC, a prosperous city that produces nothing and consumes much. The three wealthiest counties in America are DC suburbs. The global financial markets are an abstraction to Washington Beltway types. At least in most other countries, the political capital and financial center tend to be in the same place. Bankers and politicians mix daily in London, Paris, and Tokyo. For Washington, New York may as well be Mars. The regulatory state does not feel the pulse of the markets; it feels the pulse of Congress and the lawyer lobbyist hired by the interest groups. A successful regulatory body does enough to convince Congress that it deserves a bigger budget, takes care to keep the folks it regulates healthy and happy, and tries to avoid big messes it can be blamed for causing or not preventing. Everything else is beside the point. This does not mean that the regulatory state lacks dedicated and hardworking public servants. It means that their job is made hellishly difficult by conflicting forces pursuing their own agendas.

The regulated, by contrast, have a straightforward agenda. They need to make as much money as they can to satisfy their institutional investors. Laws and regulations are simply an obstacle course they navigate to collect $200 and not go to jail. In fact, laws can be used creatively by business people to hamper or cripple potential competitors. In contrast, regulators do not have the resources to recruit and motivate the kind of financial and legal talent a large financial services firm can. So, these laws are a bit like placing large carnivores in a Habitrail in hopes of channeling their behavior and protecting the hamsters. Remember, you and I are at the bottom of the food chain.

UNINTENDED CONSEQUENCES

This would be bad enough if the purposes of regulation were consistent and the consequences of specific regulations were knowable. They are not. Take the example of deposit insurance, probably the worst single idea in financial regulation.

The New Deal had to cope with an epidemic of bank failures when it came into office. Setting up a fund to pay back depositors when a bank failed was an obvious way to reduce the chances of a "run" on a bank. And government guarantees, despite the evidence of real history, are remarkably soothing to bank depositors. Better still, the fund was set up so deposit insurance would be paid for by compulsory premiums paid by the industry itself. One of the genius aspects of the American regulatory state is to get public results out of private money.

However, under that system, the taxpayers remained on the hook if losses exceeded the insurance fund. As a result, the Federal Deposit Insurance Corporation (FDIC), the newfangled deposit insurance company, had to become a major bank regulator. After all, it couldn't control its losses if it couldn't tell banks to avoid risky business. It needed to collect detailed information from the insured banks on a regular basis and inspect their portfolios of loans. Of course, in doing these things, it was performing redundant inspections and paperwork already demanded by other banking supervisors like the Comptroller of the Currency (for banks with national charters) and the Federal Reserve (for state chartered banks and all bank holding companies, that is, corporations that owned banks) and banking superintendents in all fifty states.

Most banks in the United States find themselves with some sort of regulator on its premises or on the phone all the time. It is not as if nobody is paying attention. The problem is that almost all regulatory compliance is maintained by ticking boxes or filling in numbers on forms. Both the banks and regulators end up going through the motions. It is hard to name a single banking crack-up that was ever spotted and prevented by formal regulatory procedures in any jurisdiction.

MORAL HAZARD

Meanwhile, the fact that deposits are insured by the government motivates everyone from depositors to bankers to politicians to act like spoiled children instead of grown-ups. Economists call this infantilization of conduct "moral hazard." Basically, moral hazard is what happens when you remove consequences for risky behavior. If you know in advance that the judge will let you off if you are stopped for a DWI, you might be inclined to drive with a few drinks in you. If you know that nothing bad will happen to you even if you cause an accident, the temptation to party hearty may be too much.

Deposit insurance means that depositors don't have to worry about where they place their money. This is a terrible idea because, as Bagehot pointed out, banking is essentially a "privileged opportunity" to make money based on trust. Fear of losing the public's trust—what is called "reputational risk"—used to be the first line of defense against bad banking practices. Before the FDIC, a smart banker would never do anything he didn't want his depositors to hear about in the news. Deposit insurance levels the playing field between good banks—of which there are many, even now—and bad banks. It takes away the consumers' key responsibility for their own money, which is to do business only with people they know and trust.

For bankers, deposit insurance is pretty much an inducement to take reckless bets using OPM. It guarantees that, provided the bank is large enough, government cannot really afford to let it collapse. There is an old saying attributed to Keynes that if I owe my bank manager a thousand pounds, I am at his mercy, but if I owe him a million pounds, our positions are reversed. A deposit protection scheme that only covers small savers up to a few thousand dollars would protect almost all bank retail customers. Few of us can save more than that. Deposit insurance that covers $100,000 on each account or more—we are now up to $250,000—is an open invitation to institutional money seeking high returns at no risk. It puts the government on the hook for so much cash that the government finds itself at the mercy of the bank. That is why the FDIC has a very good process and track record at shutting down and "resolving" small banks that get themselves into trouble. They can afford it, and the little bank holds no hostages so has no power to negotiate. For large banks, deposit insurance gives them confidence that they will be bailed out if things go south because they are just too big to be "resolved" in the normal FDIC process. This turns into a "heads I win, tails I don't lose" situation that encourages risky bets with OPM. Everyone in finance, academia, and the regulatory world knows this, but getting deposit insurance

down to a level that only small savers are protected is off the legislative table. This is because the politicians come into the picture.

CASHING IN

The expansion of deposit insurance is essentially a free goodie that
politicians can get credit for and never expect to pay for in tax dollars.
Who can object to providing yet more protection for consumers,
especially if banks pay the premiums? The worst financial crisis in
post-war U.S. history until the current one was triggered by Congress
passing the Garn-St. Germain Act of 1982. Back in those innocent
times, most mortgages were made by savings and loan institutions
and were funded by savings accounts. The amount of interest that
banks could pay was still capped by a New Deal-era rule called Regulation Q. The savings banks had a built-in $1/4$% advantage over bank
rates. The Great Inflation of the late 1970s and a series of steep interest rate hikes that the heroic Fed Chairman, Paul Volcker, used to
break inflation's back made regulated rates a bad joke. If you kept
your money in a passbook account paying 5%, you saw it melt away
amid 17% inflation. Silly regulations create opportunities for the
unregulated at all times and in all places.

The bright people at Merrill Lynch, a stock broker regulated by
the Securities Exchange Commission and in theory unable to take
deposits from the public, hit pay dirt in this situation. They invented
the money market account (MMA), something no politician or regulator had foreseen. Essentially, a money market account is a share in a
money market fund that invests in short-term money market paper
like negotiable CDs, commercial paper, and bankers' acceptances.
These instruments paid real market rates that were much, much
higher than regulated bank rates. To make the MMA really useful to
ordinary bank customers, all Merrill needed to do was find a friendly
bank to offer checking services for these accounts. The combination
of unregulated market returns and checking was unbeatable. The best
alternative thrifts and banks could offer was a negotiable order of
withdrawal or NOW account, essentially a checkable savings account.

Funds flowed out of thrifts and banks at such a rate that at one
point MMA balances actually exceeded those in regulated consumer
checking accounts. It was the beginning of a shift of the household

balance sheet out of banks and thrifts and into market investments that lasted up to the current crisis.

The immediate problem was that the thrift industry could not fund new mortgages. Anything that harms the housing industry gets the attention of Congress. A sensible person would think that the answer was simple: Just deregulate interest rates. To its credit, Congress did that in the Garn-St. Germain Act, largely at the behest of the thrift and bank lobbies. However, this was done without much thought as to what thrifts and banks could safely do with high-interest deposits. Worse, in the dead of night, Congressman St. Germain slipped a provision into the bill raising the limits on deposit insurance from $10,000 per depositor to $100,000.

This was the equivalent of giving whiskey and car keys to teenage boys. The massive amount of money the banks and thrifts attracted using market rates and essentially unlimited FDIC insurance (a big investor could open many $100,000 accounts) was an accident waiting to happen. Small banks and thrifts became involved in high-risk, high-return lending, especially commercial real estate projects, because thrifts were still restricted from most business lending and high mortgage rates held down consumer demand. Real history shows that real estate or "property" lending is more or less the most dangerous thing a bank can do. American conditions made things worse. The industry contained thousands of small banks and thrifts that were easily bought or controlled by local real estate speculators. The classic case was that "Billy-Bob Bank" would be owned by the same investors who controlled Billy-Bob Enterprises, which owned Billy-Bob Development Corp, whose principal asset was the Billy-Bob Bank building in the Billy Bob Mall. This sort of thing was especially common in the red-hot real estate markets of the Sunbelt states, especially Texas. The Billy-Bobs in question were always big political contributors to friendly folks in Congress.

BILLY BOB BANK GOES BUST

The Billy Bob Bank boom led to the worst single financial disaster in U.S. banking history, up to the one we are now living through. The politicians at the federal and state level kept leaning on the regulators to show forbearance until real estate prices bounced back. They didn't, especially in markets where speculation had run wild. Meanwhile, the thrift industry deposit insurance fund was going broke.

Eventually, in 1989—that is, many years into the crisis—Congress passed a bill to clean up the mess called the Financial Institutions Reform, Recovery and Enforcement Act and put the FDIC in charge of insuring thrift deposits. The pet thrift regulator was replaced by a new body with real teeth. Above all, an independent body called the Resolution Trust Corporation (RTC) was set up by Congress to "resolve" thrifts—that is, shut them down, sell off their assets, and pay off their depositors—using taxpayer money. The process was long and messy. By 2000, nearly 3,000 banks and thrifts had been put out of their misery at a final cost estimated by the FDIC of $153 billion. These were almost all small institutions (total assets of about half a trillion dollars), so the impact on the financial system was not catastrophic except at a local level. States like Texas and regions like New England lost the bulk of their local banks, with predictable results on economic activity. Technically, the RTC eventually turned a paper profit on its asset disposals, but few would suggest that this was a brilliant use of taxpayer money. Billy Bob, by the way, was last seen in Washington promoting Green energy.

THE BIG SHAKE DOWN

If government regulation is pretty bad at preventing problems that are basically structural, its record on consumer protection is even worse. With only a handful of exceptions, Congress has no interest in how banking and finance really work. It has come to view the financial services industry as a money tree it can shake to buy votes and enlist special interest groups as political foot soldiers. The worst example of this is the Community Reinvestment Act, or CRA, which was cooked up under Jimmy Carter. It starts with the presumption that banks discriminate against minority communities. While there is some ugly history to support this view, in fact, banks discriminate against all people with low incomes because it is hard to make money serving them. CRA legislation forced the Federal Reserve to hold hearings every time a bank wanted to open or close a branch and take into account how much low-income and minority lending a bank was doing. This process empowered "community organizers" and left-wing activist groups like Association of Community Organizations for Reform Now (ACORN) to make angry protests until they were bought off by having money funneled through them and their allies. Banks basically wrote this money off the second it went out the door as a cost of doing business. Congress was not very curious about where the money went either. In a normal country, the government provides low-cost financial services to the lower-income segments through post office banking and public savings banks. CRA, however, wasn't about providing services. It was a shakedown that funded core constituents of the Democratic Party with bank shareholder money.

THE AFFORDABLE HOUSING SCAM

The proximate cause of the financial market meltdown was pressure from the ACORNs of this world and the Clinton administration for both banks and government-sponsored enterprises (GSEs, i.e., Fannie Mae and Freddie Mac) to loosen their credit standards for residential mortgages to the point that virtually anyone could get a mortgage. The Bush administration followed along the same lines and legislators of both parties pointed with pride as the percentage of Americans owning their own homes kept climbing toward 65%. This could only be done by stretching the structured finance sausage machine to the breaking point and allowing the GSEs to take on mind-blowing amounts of risk. They pumped their combined balance sheets up to half the size of the GDP. They lost all internal control. Their defenders in Congress, including the current chairmen of the House and Senate Banking Committees and the current President, stiff-armed all attempts to bring the GSEs under effective regulation.

The rest is history. The key point is that given the historical nature of American politics, especially the two-year Congressional election cycle, the mix of politics and finance is always going to be toxic and dangerous to the taxpayer.

7

▼

The Natural History of Financial Folly

DULL MARKETS

We keep insisting that the greatest writer on banking and finance was Walter Bagehot. One of the best chapter titles he ever wrote was "Why Lombard Street is often very dull, and sometimes extremely excited," Lombard Street being his tag for the global financial market centered in London. What Bagehot went on to describe is how, during long periods of growth and stability, players in the financial market get lulled into believing good times will go on forever. This confidence in the future will always, and in all places, lead to excessive optimism and an itch to push the envelope a bit, to "innovate" in today's jargon. The smart money will get cocky, and the dumb money will want in on the game, getting fleeced in the process. This is the dull patch. Credit standards get lax; people get less nervous about cutting a few corners. Everyone is happy, everyone is making money. Politicians take credit for a prosperity they did nothing to create (Harding and Coolidge in the 1920s, Clinton in the 1990s). Nobody wants regulators to get too nosey. Rich and successful people, even the obscenely rich and vulgar, are admired and lionized in the press.

EXCITED MARKETS

Then someone smells a rat. Usually it is noticed that the smart money did something really dumb, perhaps even crooked. Remember 2001, when we all found out that Enron, Tyco, and WorldCom were all shell games? Dull euphoria turns to panic, as both optimism and trust evaporate instantly. This is when things get extremely exciting. Everyone rushes to the exits at the same time, everyone wants cash, and nobody wants risks. Paper fortunes implode. Politicians, who understand nothing of what caused the prosperity or the panic, loudly proclaim outrage and that "something must be done." The greedy, dumb-money folks suddenly become victims. The rich become villains to be punished. Lots of show trials (also know as congressional hearings) lead to lots of poorly crafted laws and regulations— (remember when Sarbanes-Oxley was supposed to fix everything?)— that almost always make things worse. Central banks pump up the money supply and slash interest rates to restore investor confidence and halt the crisis. Things bottom out. Back to dull.

THEY CAN'T HELP THEMSELVES

This movie has played longer than *The Rocky Horror Picture Show.* The economist Charles Kindleberger's book, *Manias, Panics and Crashes,* is classic history of financial train wrecks that everyone should read. Briefer and more amusingly, Charles Mackay, a clear-eyed Scotsman, wrote sketches on some of the biggest bubbles and panics of the seventeenth and eighteenth centuries in the book, *Great Popular Delusions and the Madness of Crowds* (1841).

What both authors recognize, along with Bagehot and other wise students of markets, is that markets are neither good nor bad. They are what they are, the only mechanism for "discovering prices" and swapping stuff that has ever been shown to work. Markets do always work, after a fashion, but they are neither *rational* nor *efficient* (something modern economists somehow talked themselves into believing). They are profoundly social, starting with the village fair and extending into high-tech electronic trading floors. Human beings are deeply social animals, needing and wanting to belong to a group. We get carried along by collective emotions. These can degenerate into mindless mob psychology very easily. The dull euphoria of a market entranced by the commercial possibilities of the internet can quite quickly morph into a full-blown mania like the dot.com boom of the 1990s.

THE FIRST BUBBLE

Everybody who has even a passing interest in economic history has a favorite folly. I confess that the South Sea Bubble of the 1720s is my own top pick, although the extraordinary adventures of the Scots financier John Law in France during the same period makes for even more exciting reading in Ferguson's hands. In London, bubble mania even swept up Sir Isaac Newton, perhaps the smartest man who ever lived. (While most of us struggled with calculus in school, he largely invented it from scratch.) Like most of the dot.com stocks of the 1990s, the South Sea Company was a company that important people said would make a fortune without ever being quite able to explain how (the story kept changing, from the Latin American slave trade to government debt refinancing, and it never really did much or showed a profit). But everybody wanted in because the stock price kept climbing, and it kept climbing because everyone wanted in. People coined the term "bubble" to describe how the stock's price kept inflating. Some may have hoped they could get out before it popped; others were so impressed by the company's board, its connections, and who was buying the stock that they thought it must be a winner even if they couldn't say at what game.

Sir Isaac was the last guy you would expect to get caught. Newton had been knighted by Queen Anne for his contributions to science, the first man so honored. He was Astronomer Royal, Master of the Royal Mint (an early gold standard fan) and a math and physics wiz at Cambridge University. He jumped into the South Sea Company stock like everybody else. He made a bundle and got out of the stock. The South Sea stock kept climbing and climbing some more. Sir Isaac just couldn't stay out. He went back in at a much higher price, just in time to lose a fortune when the South Sea Company collapsed.

THE MADNESS OF CROWDS

Moral of the story: Manias and bubbles are products of emotions and mob psychology that even the most rational and intelligent of us cannot resist. The secondary moral is that big manias and bubbles, when they burst, cause wild overreactions. Things go from everything looking golden to everything looking like trash in an instant. The real danger is that of a backlash against the markets rather than against the bad actors that crossed the line during the mania.

THE CYNICISM OF POLITICS

Disgraced New York Governor Eliot Spitzer rose to power by abusing the power of his office as state Attorney General to conduct a series of vicious prosecutions by way of press conference (he never brought and sustained a single real criminal case). Fear of this tactic allowed him to shake down Wall Street for big cash settlements in the wake of the dot.com crash. It was pure political opportunism; it is hard to see how anyone benefited other than him. The man the press dubbed the "Sheriff of Wall Street" did nothing to head off the excesses behind the bubble in asset-backed securities that brought down Wall Street in 2008. In fact, by vindictively driving the one man from power who really understood AIG and who essentially managed its risk, its founder Hank Greenburg, Spitzer bears at least some responsibility for destabilizing a critical cog in the credit default swap market on the eve of the crisis. AIG's default book may have proved fatal in any case but Spitzer weakened the company by arbitrarily using an arcane state law to undermine other key parts of its global business model such as finite risk contracts, a key product in the global reinsurance market. He has nonetheless set a useful example for state attorney generals everywhere, including in Massachusetts, which got a big settlement from Goldman in 2009 without even bothering to bring a complaint.

And we can expect more of this stuff too, all of which is good for pols but full of bad unintended consequences. For example, the British government passed the Bubble Act in 1720, supposedly to prevent speculation but actually to help prop up the South Sea share price. The unintended effect of the Act was to make it almost impossible for people to form new joint-stock companies in England for over a century, something that helped the United States, where incorporation was relatively easy to eventually overtake British industry. Rushing to push through "tough" reforms after the public gets angry at business and finance is always extremely good politics but very bad government.

We find ourselves at a similar fork in the road today. In the 2008 election, both candidates showed absolutely no understanding of the roots of the bubble, and both were, to one degree or another, quite happy to put the market on trial. We can't know how the current remake of this movie will end, but if politics plays out as usual in Washington, we cannot expect a happy one.

THE USE OF PANICS

Panics, however, do have their uses. If the two dominant moods of the financial markets are fear and greed, human beings are perfectly capable of learning from experience. Fear does not go away with experience, it gets tempered. Combat veterans make good troops not because they are braver but because they know what to expect. In the classical period of the global financial market, the age of the gold standard between 1873 and 1914, stock market crashes and panics were fairly frequent. They were normal market events. Anyone who went to work in the City of London or Wall Street was a virgin until he lived through one of them. The crises would always burn themselves out, often with little or no government involvement. Buying and selling would resume, and life would go on. In short, everyone accepted that the system had to purge itself of its excesses. The credit system might have gotten a bit infected by overconfidence and loose standards, but the occasional bust (and these things happened every few years) prevented it from becoming a life-threatening pathogen. Firms and individuals who had over-borrowed or over-traded paid the price and either failed or were taken over by more sober rivals. Reputation was cultivated as a strength. Prudence and fair dealing built wealth. In other words, frequent booms and busts created market discipline and sorted out who the strong, long-term players really were. Markets healed themselves.

WHY THINGS ARE WORSE THIS TIME

The global financial market collapse that started in 2008 is vastly larger in scale and scope and has progressed with far greater speed than even the legendary crash of 1929. The depths and duration of the damage inflicted on the global economy may well be substantially worse than the results of that earlier event for one simple reason: For over a generation, we have refused to let market busts play themselves out. This has been called the "Great Moderation." Between 1982, when the ruinous inflation set off by the Great Society and Vietnam War spending of Lyndon Johnson in the late sixties had finally been broken by Paul Volcker's Federal Reserve, and the credit market crisis of the summer of 2008, the global financial markets went from strength to strength for a quarter century. Not that there were not crises—there were, including whoppers like the U.S. Savings and Loan industry meltdown or the dot.com crash. However, the markets came to *expect* to be bailed out by the government, specifically by the Federal Reserve under the legendary Alan Greenspan, who presided over the Fed for 18 of these 25 years. The financial world came to believe that Uncle Alan would always bail them out. The markets also came to believe in the existence of a "plunge prevention committee" that included key figures from Wall Street and the federal government. The Plunge Prevention Committee (PPC) would pull strings to prevent any hiccup in the markets from turning into a real long-term bust. And, true or not, these beliefs were vindicated by events.

The federal government opened its check book in the 1980s to clean up the Savings and Loan mess, after fudging its regulatory rules and using its credit to get the largest U.S. banks out of their bad loans to Latin American and other developing countries. The Fed flooded the banks with money to restore confidence after the 1987 stock market crash, preventing a real turn down in the economy. It engineered a bail-out of Mexico in 1994, and with the International Monetary Fund helped stopped a global market panic after the Asian currency crisis of 1997. It flooded the markets with cheap money after the dot.com bubble bust at the end of 2000 and again after September 11, 2001. The Fed even pumped money into the system to prevent the phony crisis of Y2K, the idea that the world's computers would go wacky when the calendar rolled over into the New Millennium on January 1, 2000. By and large, all these actions were successful. Nobody could really ask if they were proper or necessary because of the record of success. Over time, the Great Moderation began to take the fear out of the equation for financial market players. That left only greed.

BANKERS GONE WILD

If there is one constant that runs through the work of Walter Bagehot it is that banking is a simple business that needs to follow simple rules. Innovation usually amounts to forgetting the rules (or having never learned them) and always ends up in tears. For this reason, he felt that dull, and even stupid men, were far better bankers than people who were clever. The decline of wholesome fear during the Great Moderation was probably not enough to turn credit from the wholesome lifeblood of an economy into a pathogen. A panic within the financial markets as they existed in 1982, if based on overconfidence built up over 25 years, would be pretty nasty. However, over the same period of time, the structure of the financial markets has been transformed beyond recognition. Bagehot must be spinning in his grave at how "innovation" has run wild in finance.

THE LONG ROAD TO FINANCIAL PERDITION

The 1929 crash and subsequent depression allowed the New Dealers and populists in Washington to put the U.S. financial system into a regulatory straitjacket for fifty years. Congress is very good at doing this sort of thing and very bad at undoing it.

The central idea embodied in the Banking Act of 1933—better known as Glass-Steagall—was to essentially ring-fence the financial industry into separate corals, each with a different set of cowboys and sheriffs in charge. Banks were excluded from the securities business. They could only take deposits and make loans and were heavily regulated in a crazy quilt way that reflected political reality. The Federal Deposit Insurance Corporation inspected the banks it insured. The Comptroller of the Currency, a relic of the 1864 Bank Act, continued to ride herd on the national banks. The states all had their own bank chartering processes and regulators, but the Fed rode herd on the states banks who were members, and later when banks were allowed to form holding companies it rode herd on those as well. Banks, could, and did, switch between national and state charters. Nobody coordinated any of these bodies; all had their friends in Congress and the statehouses.

Securities firms were defined as licensed "broker dealers" who could both underwrite stocks and bonds and trade them, both for customers and on their own account. They were not allowed near lending and deposits. A new sheriff, the Securities and Exchange Commission (SEC), rode herd on them, enforcing a new raft of securities laws and regulations aimed at preventing the abuses that politicians believed had caused the 1929 crash. The SEC had almost no contact with the regulatory bodies mentioned above, and in time developed its own following on Capitol Hill. The states had their own securities laws and regulators, needless to say. States also regulated the insurance industry and many other institutional investors like mutual funds.

The New Deal also took steps to funnel the nation's savings into the least productive use of capital: Housing. To understand New Deal thinking, you need to remember *It's a Wonderful Life*. George Bailey is the acceptable face of finance; he takes care of people's savings and lets the little guy move up in the world and live the American Dream by owning his own home. Banker Potter is a greedy slum lord. Congress believed that home ownership was so important that it required a financial industry of its own. First, it established a favorable charter for savings banks with their own, somewhat indulgent regulator. It also got the U.S. Post Office out of the savings bank business, making America one of the few countries where postal banks do not provide basic savings and payment services. Second, by making mortgage interest an income tax deduction, they made building up equity in a home one of the few ways ordinary people could accumulate retirement savings. Third, they created a government-run secondary market in mortgages through Federal Home Loan Banks. These were later joined by the GSEs (Fannie Mae and Freddie Mac) we met in Chapter Three. This housing finance industry had its own regulatory machinery and its own friends in Congress. No other country has such a mortgage industry so deeply entwined in partisan politics.

U.S. BANKING IN "THE ERA OF THREE-SIX-THREE"

When the Banking Act of 1933 forced the blue-blood of all U.S. Banks to choose between a commercial banking charter and a broker-dealer charter, J.P. Morgan chose to be a bank in a heartbeat. Its securities business was spun off as Morgan Stanley and Company. Other banks followed suit. The securities markets of the New Deal era were terrible places to be. The investor class was badly hit by the crash and then targeted by New Deal taxes. The stock market was on life support for a decade and then recovered slowly into the 1950s. Corporations mainly borrowed from the commercial banks

Thus was born the "rule of 3-6-3" for banking success: Pay 3% interest to depositors, charge 6% to borrowers, and be at the country club for a 3 o'clock tee time. Bankers were the custodians of public institutions, were public utilities in fact, and acted accordingly. They were not especially well paid, but were completely secure in their employment compared with mere businessmen They were genteel, civic-minded, golf-playing, and extremely risk averse. There is a famous anecdote in Martin Meyer's classic account *The Bankers* where an old gentleman who was retiring from a Virginia bank during the 1970s was asked what the greatest change he had seen in his long career. His answer: "Air conditioning."

THE TERM LOAN IS BORN

Despite Congress's attempt to make banking a public utility, the era of 3-6-3 saw fundamental changes in U.S. banking. The first of these was the term loan. This was invented back in the 1920s by a very bright young Russian émigré named Serge Semenenko, who worked for the First National Bank of Boston. He came up with the idea of making loans for much longer periods of time than traditional working capital loans to "special industries" that did not fit the mold of bond markets or traditional banking. These included the new Hollywood movie industry, trucking, airlines, and hotel chains.

Term loans introduced a new tool called "cash flow analysis" to banking. The risk of a loan was predicted based on the likely future cash flow of a company based on past financial statements. If over the last three or four years, a company's sales had turned into receivables at a certain rate, its receivables had turned into cash at a certain rate, and its cash outflows for other things like interest and taxes were in a certain range, something called "free cash flow" could be determined by simple math. If all things remain more or less equal, a banker who does the math should be able to calculate how much a borrower can afford to pay back in principal and interest on borrowed money. Of course, all things are rarely equal for any period of time.

With the term loan, U.S. banks had committed the original sin of believing that math—what they chose to call "credit analysis"—would allow them to predict the future beyond a few hundred days.

BANK ACCOUNTS FOR EVERYONE

The 1950s and 1960s also saw a vast migration to the suburbs and with it the expansion of the "middle class." Americans of working-class backgrounds were fast becoming prosperous as employment, wages, and home ownership soared. Bank checking accounts became part of everyday life for the majority of American families during these decades. Consumer deposits fed the 3-6-3 machine's hunger for OPM, but there were never enough deposits. They were also costly, since millions of small accounts writing billions of checks caused a big jump in bank employees and branch locations. In fact, simply processing paper checks became the largest single expense in the banking system as America went from a country where most people were paid in cash and spent cash to a country where most folks had a deposit money account all in a single generation.

These checking deposits, however, were not in the big money center banks but were spread over 27,000 banks and thousand of credit unions and "thrifts" because of state and federal restrictions on state-wide and interstate banking.

CORRESPONDENT BANKING

Big banks, therefore, figured out how to grow their stash of OPM by tapping into the surge in retail deposits indirectly. First, the surge in check payments caused more money to gush through the correspondent banking system. The banks that sat in the big national clearing house cities like New York and Chicago competed for the clearing business of regional banks in places like Cleveland, which in turn served the needs of local banks in small towns across Ohio. All these services were paid for by "compensating balances." This means that downstream banks on Main Street left extra cash balances with their big city correspondent, over and above the funds needed to make their customer payments, as a payment "in kind" for a whole raft of services. Even corporate customers got hit with "compensating balances" requirements to secure access to loans and lines of credit. Still, the banks' hunger for OPM went unsatisfied as loan demand continued to grow through the 1960s economic boom. Something more was needed.

THE CD IS BORN

The answer was simply buying OPM in the open market. Unlike checking accounts or compensating balances that were tied to real customers and their payments, market funding was in principle unlimited. In 1961, a banker named Walt Wriston at the First National City Bank of New York invented the certificate of deposit or "CD."

Today every granny in Miami is an expert in comparing CD rates, but few people understand it for the radical departure it really was. The CD is an IOU that a bank sells for cash that a buyer locks up for a fixed period of time, say six months or eighteen months, at a fixed rate of interest. At first, CDs were limited to corporations with extra money to park in minimum amounts of $100,000, roughly a million dollars in today's money. The CD was a *negotiable* instrument. If a big corporation bought a CD for six months and suddenly needed the cash, it could sell its claim to be repaid with interest to another investor.

CDs for the general public followed a decade later. Retail CDs, of course, took advantage of Federal Deposit Insurance and the legislated inability of commercial banks to pay anything like market rates of interest. Over time, CDs became the equal of checking accounts as a source of funds for banks. In theory, as long as they could issue CDs at lower rates than they could lend, banks could be lenders without being big retail deposit takers.

LEND LONG, BORROW SHORT

It was then but a short step to adopt the dark arts of asset and liability management, or ALM—specifically, the game of mismatching loans and deposits. Remember, banks traditionally had to lend short because their depositors could demand cash at any time. The new term loans could run for several years. If a bank adopted "matched funding," it would issue 24-month CDs to fund a 24-month loan, and three-year CDs to fund a three-year loan and so on. Of course, it would soon discover that the market price for 24-month money was roughly the same whether a company was borrowing it or a bank was. A regulated bank would normally have some price advantage over the average company, but normally not enough to make fat profits. However, if the bank were really clever, it could keep its funding on the short side, say by having a lot of overnight federal funds and six-month CDs in the mix. Since time is risk, it would be paying lower interest rates than it would by match funding.

As banks came to understand this, a market in big-ticket "wholesale" deposits developed nationally and internationally. On the sell side would be investors with spare cash to park, and on the buy side would be the banks needing to fund loans for various periods. This interbank market allowed banks to deliberately "mismatch" their balance sheets—lend long and fund short. As long as very short-term borrowing could always be "rolled-over" into new borrowings, banks with the boldest mismatch stood to make the most money on their loans.

This strategy assumed the interbank market would always be there. By the 1970s, only a few old-fashioned bankers worried about such things. They thought that mismatched funding was an accident waiting to happen. However, the game had changed, and no modern banker thought that you actually had to have deposits to make loans safely. Until, that is, the summer of 2007, when the interbank market froze up and our current financial crisis began.

FINANCE RETURNS TO LONDON

The first sign that the global financial system was falling apart came in the freezing up of the London interbank market in August of 2007. LIBOR—the London Interbank Offered Rate, essentially the rate at which banks will offer to lend to other banks for various periods— went through the roof. The first question that springs to mind is, "Why is the global market in dollar deposits in London anyway"?

This is due to yet another accident of history with big consequences, this time Kennedy Administration policies. In the 1960s, U.S. firms were rapidly expanding their operations overseas as Europe boomed. These overseas operations continued to raise financing in the United States. The Kennedy Administration thought this was a bad thing for the U.S. economy, so in 1963 it passed the Interest Equalization Tax, or IET, which charged U.S. lenders 15% on all interest received from overseas borrowers.

Naturally, big U.S. banks still wanted to serve their largest corporate customers as they expanded abroad. Foreign banks were in no position to lend dollars. These factors, along with the Cold War, led to the accidental creation of the Eurodollar market, a key milestone in the road to the re-emergence of a truly integrated global financial system for the first time since the outbreak of World War I in August 1914.

WHY LONDON

In the early 1960s, London as a financial center was a shadow of its former self. The two world wars had reduced Britain from being a country everyone owed money into a country that struggled to pay its bills. Exchange controls imposed when war broke out in 1939 were still in place. Sterling was no longer pegged to gold, and the U.S. dollar had replaced it as the world currency. The British economy was one of the weakest in Europe, saddled with sky-high taxes to support an unaffordable welfare state.

Despite that, London retained some key advantages as a place to do international business. First, like the United States, the language of business was English. But unlike the United States, where Congress could and did make destructive laws like the IET all the time, banking and finance were virtually unregulated aside from the oversight of the Bank of England. London also had centuries of proven commitment to protecting the money and the rights of foreigners who did business there. The U.K. had a simple, fair, expedient, and affordable legal system compared with the capricious and exorbitant morass of state and federal courts in the United States. Centuries of financial leadership had produced a deep London labor pool of financial professionals. All London lacked was a big pool of the key global currency, the U.S. dollar.

OFFSHORE MONEY

How can a pool of money denominated in U.S. dollars exist in a foreign capital? Certainly the notion never occurred to U.S. regulators and politicians, since foreign currency accounts are still unknown here. However, like many things in banking and finance, the United States is the odd man out. Foreign currency accounts had long been available in London and other global financial hubs. These were not accounts that allowed you to take U.S. dollars out of an ATM and spend it in London. Currency notes and coin obviously only work in places where they are legal tender. I can't buy a pizza with the ten pound note in the back of my wallet. However, if I live in London, it is perfectly possible for me to have a local bank account in dollars (or euros, or almost any other currency that can be converted). All this means is my dollar account in London is, like any deposit money account, a claim on dollars held in the U.S. banking system. I can convert this claim into local currency—sterling in this case—by selling dollars for sterling. But I can also use the dollars in London by lending them to someone who needs U.S. dollars to make a payment or pay a debt.

THE BIRTH OF THE EURODOLLAR

In the post-war era, the Soviet Union and other communist countries in Europe held substantial U.S. dollar assets in U.S. banks. This persisted until the Kennedy era, despite the onset of the Cold War. The escalation of tensions that culminated in the Cuban Missile Crisis changed this. The Soviets feared that the Americans might simply steal their dollars and moved them into the London branch of a bank they controlled called Eurobank. The dollars parked there became known as Eurodollars. This pool dollars presented an opportunity to make dollar loans free of the politics and regulations of the United States but within the clubby rules of London.

Soon the Eurodollar became the fuel for restoring London to its pre-1914 status as the financial capital of the world. This required that the U.S. banks get into the game. They did. A legendary Greek financier named Minos Zombinakis got the stodgy Manufacturers Hanover, a leading New York bank of the time, to set up a London merchant bank. Michael Von Clemm, a protégé of Walt Wriston, started a dollar certificate of deposit market in London. Soon the market in interbank deposits in London exceeded both the U.K. sterling market and the dollar market in New York. U.S. and foreign banks swarmed to London. By the 1970s, there were hundreds of foreign banks doing business in London, almost all of it Eurodollar business. There was nothing to keep them out, since British banking had never been regulated in a formal sense. Since they were not doing local sterling business, all the banks required was a foreign exchange license from the Bank of England.

BOOM TIMES IN LONDON

In the early days, the business of the Eurodollar markets could not be simpler. Foreigners with big dollar income streams such as petroleum-exporting countries would deposit these funds in the biggest, safest U.S. bank branches in London. These banks would resell excess deposits to other banks in the market. The funds would be used for large, multi-year loans to foreign governments, government enterprises, and corporations. Some of this was deficit financing by governments that couldn't borrow in their home markets. Much of it was borrowing dollars in London to buy oil from countries that would just deposit the proceeds in London. However, things like the highway systems of Italy and Spain were built on Eurodollar loans. Loans got larger, longer, and more complex, just as the term loan market had in the United States. Like there, it became typical for a "lead" bank to put a deal together and "syndicate" it to a club of other banks, getting fees in the process while reducing its risks. The market was soon dominated by the big American international banks. By the time Washington D.C. figured out that the most important dollar financing market in the world had ended up in London, it was too late. The IET was repealed in 1974, but the global dollar market never really came back to New York

U.S. BANKERS LEARN A DANGEROUS GAME

The Eurodollar market was a golden opportunity for the top U.S. banks to escape the jail set up for them by Glass-Steagall.

It was also dangerous. The Eurodollar market in London had only the most flimsy linkage to the U.S. domestic banking system and money markets. It had no real linkage to the banking system and money market of its host country. It may as well have existed on the moon. In fact, it set the fashion for "off-shore" banking and financial centers. Places like Nassau, Bahamas, Grand Cayman, The Dutch Antilles, Bermuda, and Luxembourg all became home to hundreds of companies set up by major banks and corporations to avoid taxation and onerous regulations at home. Most of these were little more than brass plates on a law office or accountant's door, and if addresses on the moon had been available, they no doubt would have been used as well.

MARKETS WITHOUT COUNTRIES

Stateless global markets worked fine as long as there was no system-wide banking panic like that which broke out in the summer of 2007. Now, suddenly, Bagehot's key notion that banking markets can only be stabilized by a "lender of last resort"—a central bank or the equivalent in a clearing house—has come home. The global "financial economy" has become, over a generation, vastly greater in size than even the largest economies like the United States and Japan. Nobody has the resources to stop a panic in the classic sense, least of all the offshore banking centers. Since their birth, the Euromarkets have grown much faster than both the "real" global economy and the financial economy of individual states. This swelling of the sheer scale of the global financial economy was possible because banking in the Euromarkets gradually became almost purely concerned with trading in financial instruments unlinked to the real economy of buying and selling stuff. The bankers in the Euromarkets effectively had no constraints.

All a bank needed was highly skilled (or lucky) traders. No pesky customers were needed for deposits—you simply bought OPM in the interbank market. The benchmark rate became know as LIBOR—the London Interbank Offered Rate—and remains the most important single interest rate in the financial world. This is why, when LIBOR went through the roof in August 2007, it was the canary in the mineshaft signaling the start of a global credit crunch that morphed into a full-fledged crisis: Interbank lending had seized up because banks wouldn't trust each other with even short-term placements. This was a shock from which the system only recovered slowly and tentatively.

DANGEROUS CUSTOMERS

The third source of danger for bankers gone wild was keeping bad company. Governments or government enterprises from the very beginning of the Euromarkets were vastly more important than other borrowers. Minos Zombinakis made his first Eurodollar loan to the Shah of Iran. Iran was also a big depositor in the market. Sigmund Warburg made the first Eurodollar loan to Italy.

This at first blush seems natural enough. After all, London merchant bankers had been raising money for sovereigns since the time of the Rothschild's. However, those loans were in the form of foreign bonds sold to wealthy investors who accepted the risk. Bank lending to a government means giving depositors money to a borrower that doesn't have to pay it back. Governments have something called "sovereign immunity," which means that they don't have to defend their actions in court. Unlike you and me, governments can legally walk away from debts they owe their own citizens or anyone else. At worst, a government that refuses to pay its debts only harms its ability to borrow again. Many countries borrowing in the Euromarket couldn't sell bonds because of past repudiation of debt.

COUNTRIES DON'T GO BANKRUPT

So why were U.S. banks willing to make hundreds of billions in loans to foreign governments that in many cases couldn't even get their own citizens to buy their bonds? The simple answer is that they needed the profits that 3-6-3 banking couldn't supply. Walter Wriston, at that point head of the biggest U.S. bank, famously said that "countries do not go bankrupt." This was narrowly true but false in substance. Of course, countries do not go "bankrupt" because they are beyond the law. On the other hand, real history shows that countries almost never pay their debts. Either they simply default, or they debase their currencies through inflation, or they issue more debt to pay off older bonds. So why did everyone believe Wriston? Because banking is a business in which you can never lose your job for doing

what all the other boys and girls are doing. Wriston was a conspicuous success. So was his bank. No big-time banker could "just say no"
to the sovereign lending and be certain of keeping his job.

DISINTERMEDIATION BITES

One of the reasons that the largest U.S. banks turned to the Euromarkets for profit growth in the 1960s and 1970s was simply that the 3-6-3
business back home was getting killed. This was occurring for two reasons. First, Wall Street had made a comeback in the post-war decade
and with it came more corporate bonds and equity financing for big
companies. Second, the commercial paper market began to recover
after nearly disappearing in the 1930s, and it offered a non-bank source
of financing that was often cheaper than bank loans for companies with
good credit. Banks responded by taking more risks in areas like commercial real estate to cope with "disintermediation" of their core
commercial loan business. They were setting themselves up for a fall.

THE GREAT INFLATION

In the 1970s, the world suffered a financial disaster of epic proportions and global scope known as the Great Inflation. If it was great
and a disaster, why haven't you heard of it? We are all taught in school
about the Great Depression or at least have heard the term. The Great
Inflation is usually passed over in silence but in many ways was as
equally destructive of the economic, political, and social order needed
to live our lives. For our story, however, it is stage center because end-
ing the Great Inflation led directly to the so-called Great Moderation,
the twenty-five fat years that led up to our over-leveraged and fragile
finance-driven economy. More important still, the Great Inflation
changed the world of money, banking, and finance, wiping away 3-6-3
banking and replacing it with the "market-based" banking model that
utterly transformed the real economy worldwide.

THE EVILS OF INFLATION

There is still a lot of debate among economists about the causes of the
Great Inflation. U.S. politics and policy making at the Federal Reserve

are both prime suspects, so the subject is controversial. The basic facts are simple enough. In the year 1960, consumer prices rose by 1.4%, but the rate of increase grew, slowly at first, until by 1979, prices had increased by 13.3%. At 13.3%, the value of the dollar is cut in half every five years or so. Remember, money is just another kind of stuff, but it is the stuff we use to buy everything else. Therefore, we lose the ability to plan and save for the future when its value drains away at such a rate. This is true for businesses as well as households. Money that loses its value at a high rate represents a breach of faith between the government that issues the money and the public. Specifically, it robs the public of their savings and the value of their pensions and investments. For people, especially the elderly, who rely on fixed incomes, it is the road to poverty.

THE CURSE OF GOOD INTENTIONS

If inflation is such a radical evil, why did governments let it get out of control? The answer can be found, as it so often is, in good intentions. The economic boom of the 1950s and 1960s had left many Americans behind. The Harvard economist John Kenneth Galbraith wrote a best seller in 1960 called *The Affluent Society* that painted America as a land of private wealth and public squalor. The obvious remedy was more government spending using the tools of Keynesian economics.

The U.S. economics profession as a whole had come to the consensus that it was possible to flatten the business cycle by "fine tuning" the economy through government spending. Since the best and brightest thought this could be done, it was hard to argue that it shouldn't be done. There was remarkably little resistance to the idea that the federal budget could and should run a deficit—spend more money than it took in as taxes—whenever the economy slowed down. If this meant "printing money" and a bit higher inflation for a while, so be it. Economists believed in a thing called the "Phillips Curve," which showed that the level of employment and the level of price inflation were a trade-off. If you aimed to achieve low inflation by keeping a tight lid on the supply of money, you were not providing enough juice for the economy to be running at full throttle. People who could work and wanted to work would not find jobs. If in contrast government spending "juice" was pumped in when the economy was slowing down, then you could keep the machine close to full throttle all of the time. The number of people not finding jobs would be lower. Inflation might be higher, but the extra workers' tax payments and greater output of "stuff" would keep it within acceptable bounds.

TEMPTING THE POLITICIANS

Now, this was all theory, but a theory that politicians of all stripes could love. Up until the 1960s, although politicians lived to spend taxpayer dollars, they were always inhibited by the quaint notion of a balanced budget. Franklin Roosevelt himself had qualms about the government spending money it didn't have. Even the massive effort of World War II was paid for by taxes and long-terms bonds, not by the printing press. The notion that deficit spending was positively beneficial and healthy was a little bit like the sexual revolution that occurred at the same time. What was once sinful and risky became, if not virtuous, more and more acceptable. The pill seemed to eliminate consequences for one, the science of economics for the other. The notion of virtue and the social and economic order based on virtue were swept away.

If the Great Inflation had a single author, his name is Lyndon Baines Johnson. A New Dealer to the bone and a master of getting things done in Congress, he believed there was no excuse for persistent poverty amidst plenty in a country as rich as the United States. So, he launched the Great Society and the War on Poverty, vastly increasing the size and spending of the federal government in the process. At the same time, he expanded the war in Vietnam, which he inherited from Kennedy.

This explosion in federal spending was unlike those of the Roosevelt years in one key aspect. They were not nearly as fully financed by taxation. The United States, of course, could always "print dollars," since the dollar had become the "new gold" under Bretton Woods. So, massive U.S. deficits and government borrowing could be inflated away at the expense of our trading partners and holders of U.S. bonds. The U.S. example spread to places like the U.K. that needed to kick-start sluggish economies. This was not a partisan political thing, either. Richard Nixon won power in 1968 and maintained high levels of spending on domestic programs and the Vietnam War. U.K. conservatives like Ted Heath were as addicted to spending as Labour Party governments. In 1971, Richard Nixon famously declared: "We are all Keynesians now."

THE LAST NAIL IN GOLD'S COFFIN

It was Nixon who dispensed with the last constraints of the old financial order. In 1971, the level and trend of inflation (which is to say, erosion of the real value of the dollar) had reached the point where the United States was experiencing a classic gold drain. Remember, under Bretton Woods, all currencies were pegged to the dollar and the dollar to gold. Foreign countries were getting tired of selling their stuff to the United States for dollars that kept shrinking. They increasingly demanded to convert their dollar reserves into gold. Since U.S. gold reserves were a tiny fraction of the dollars we had pumped overseas to buy everything from oil to whole companies, this could not go on very long.

Nixon's solution was to unilaterally dump the Bretton Woods system that had underpinned post-war recovery and growth. The United States severed the link between the dollar and gold by closing the "gold window" that allowed other countries to swap dollars claims for gold bullion. This was without doubt one of the greatest acts of bad faith in all financial history.

CURRENCIES FLOAT

Without the last remnant of the gold standard, the world's currencies began to "float." All countries' money was now pure "fiat money," money that was only worth something because of the power of the government over its citizens—a fiat. This meant that fiat currencies were only worth what the foreign exchange—FX in bank-speak—markets centered in London said that they were worth, not in terms of gold or some other commodity "yardstick" but in terms of each other. The FX grew very quickly and became a "professional market" only loosely tied to the real-economy requirement for foreign currency to settle debts. One real-world foreign exchange trade for a company would set off scores of trades between banks. These trades would establish the price of currencies bought and sold, both in the "spot" market (for two-day delivery) and in "forward markets (for delivery in several months or even years into the future). The forward markets allowed real-world buyers and sellers of "stuff" to buy a contract that protected them in case the currency they would need to pay or receive in the future changed value. For the professional traders at the banks, foreign exchange trading became a huge casino.

THE GATHERING STORM

Banks, especially the largest money center banks, were in an increasingly untenable position in the late 1970s and early 1980s. They had lost their high-quality, high-volume, low-risk corporate lending business to the capital markets. The industry suffered from fundamental overcapacity and could only grow profits by taking on riskier loans. This backfired badly when the Great Inflation forced the Federal Reserve to jack up interest rates, pushing many of their borrowers over the edge.

In the entire 30-year period from 1948 to 1981, the loan losses of the whole commercial banking industry had been under $30 billion. The industry lost over $45 billion in just 3 years between 1985 and l987. Between 1980 and 1992, a total of 1,142 savings and loan associations and 1,395 banks were closed, and many others were forced to merge. States as large as Texas effectively had their entire indigenous banking system fail and fall into out-of-state control. Bailouts cost the Treasury hundreds of billions, and a severe credit crunch and collapse in real estate values helped trigger and extend a recession in 1990 to 1992.

CAPITAL MARKETS TAKE OVER

The same decade that saw the banking industry enter its perfect storm saw the beginning of the longest bull market in Wall Street history.

The 25-year bull market that ended in 2008 coincides with a vast increase in pension fund assets under professional management. Some of this merely reflects demography as the Baby Boomers began to accumulate wealth. The Employee Retirement Income Security Act (ERISA) pension reforms of 1974 and the implementation of tax deferred personal pension plans, 401(k)s, in 1981 were key factors. The 1982 bipartisan commission on Social Security chaired by Alan Greenspan and Daniel Patrick Moynihan led Congress to raise payroll taxes and retirement ages in 1984, but the need for personal retirement savings became widely recognized. At the same time, corporations were anxious to shift the burden of retirement plans on to their employees. 401(k) plans are defined contribution schemes in which the plan sponsor is not responsible for providing a specified future benefit like a traditional pension. Individual retirement plan participants became responsible for the safe and sound investment of their pension assets. This created boom times in the mutual fund and insurance industries and a small army of financial planners and advisors. It also made Wall Street firms grow by leaps and bounds.

The numbers are stunning. In 1981, the Dow Jones industrial average was 875 at year end, having languished below 1,000 through most of the 1970s. By 1990, nearly 20 million employees participated in 98,000 plans with total assets of $385 billion. The Dow ended the year at 2,633.66. By 1998, there were 37 million active plan participants in 300,000 plans with total assets of $1.5 trillion. The Dow ended the year at 10,021.60. Despite the dot.com bubble bursting at the end of the millennium, the Dow closed above 14,000 in October of 2007. It was this pool of equity capital and the demanding and opportunistic institutional money managers who controlled it that forced the consolidation of an increasingly marginal U.S. banking system.

PAC-MAN BANKING

Even if the Euromarket party ended in tears with the Mexican default of 1982 and the ensuing LDC ("less developed counties," the current euphemism for poor and backward economies) debt crisis, the leading U.S. commercial banks had used the Euromarkets to escape jail and were not going back.

The LDC debt crisis of the 1980s was, however, a near-death experience (actually, several money center banks did eventually succumb from an overdose of sovereign lending). In principle, taking bond-type risk on a bank balance sheet in a competitive market was sheer folly, though to be fair the banking authorities in the United States and elsewhere encouraged this lending as an alternative to global crisis in the wake of steep increases in oil prices. In the end, the sovereign debt restructuring that saved the bulk of the money center banks converted much bank lending into so-called Brady Bonds linked to the U.S. Treasury market, the deepest and most liquid bond market in the world. Collapse of the U.S. money center banks was averted, but industry consolidation was given momentum. Not only Manufacturers Hanover, but every money center bank that was dependent on wholesale intermediation suffered in terms of earnings momentum and market value. Industry consolidation was largely a response to weakness in the traditional money center banks. By the late 1990s, only three of the top eight money center banks were still in existence as aggressive regional banks unburdened by the sins of the past began to consolidate the fragmented U.S. banking industry, with states and eventually the federal authorities easing the barriers to in-state and intrastate mergers. Had the big New York banks remained robust it is doubtful that the barriers to interstate banking and the New Deal era restrictions on bank securities activities would have been legislated away so quickly during the 1990s. Fear of their communities and businesses falling victim to evil big city bankers had caused both state legislators and Congress to maintain extremely restrictive interstate banking laws for generations. However, increasingly it became clear that the successful acquiring banks were emerging from the Heartland and the South. Traditional political opposition to nationwide banking softened, both in Congress and in state legislatures. The Billy Bob Bank fiasco had weakened so many banking systems that bilateral deals between states to allow each others banks to acquire banks and establish branches gained ground throughout the 1980s and 1990s.

Congress eventually acted to in effect regularize what had already taken place when it passed the Riegle-Neal Act in 1994 granting full nationwide branching and acquisition rights to banks. This merely accelerated a process that was in full swing.

Banks from places like Charlotte, North Carolina, Providence, Rhode Island, and Minneapolis, Minnesota grew through acquiring bank after bank, including some of the largest and oldest names in the industry. In fact, acquiring other institutions using a higher share price, quickly stripping costs out, and going after the next deal became the stock in trade of the successful "super-regional" bank. Over-paying for an acquisition or failing to successfully integrate it and squeeze out promised earnings could and did result in sudden death. The whole map of the U.S. banking industry was changed beyond recognition by a decade of eat or be eaten Pac-Man banking.

In 1984 there were 14,496 commercial banks and over 3,400 S&Ls in the FDIC insurance scheme. By year end 2008, 7,086 banks and about 1,200 thrift institutions remained. More to the point, the seven banks with over 100 billion each in deposits accounted for about 40% of all deposits and roughly half the assets in the whole banking system. These mega-banks enjoyed vast scale and market share in everything from consumer finance to corporate lending. They were, as recent events prove, almost too big to be managed safely and effectively but they were too certainly too big to be allowed to fail without risking national economic calamity. Too big to fail continues to undermine efforts at effective and equitable regulation, however what motivated the banks was earnings growth. Market cap was the key to survival and buying earnings was far easier than growing them in highly competitive markets,

Banks not only grew earnings by buying up bread and butter banking businesses but by expanding their securities businesses. The Federal Reserve was rather sympathetic to the large bank holding companies as they began to test the limits of Glass-Steagall. In 1994 the largest New York bank, much weakened by market mishaps, was purchased by a financial conglomerate that included insurance and investment banking interests under a Fed waiver. In 1999 Congress finally bit the bullet and passed the Gramm-Leach-Bliley Act driving the last nail into the coffin of New Deal banking laws. Soon almost all the major commercial banks were bulking up their investment banking businesses and in several cases becoming global players.

TOO BIG TO FAIL

Wall Street soon discovered that having a big balance sheet to lend gave their less accomplished commercial bank rivals an inside track in attracting corporate business. The most venerable Wall Street partnership, Goldman Sachs, became a public company in 1999 the last of the broker dealers to do so. Armed with big capital bases the

American investment banks increased their overseas activities and came to dominate the global capital markets from London to Asia.

The most dangerous result of the dominance of the global financial market by a handful of mostly American banks and investment banks over the last decades turned out to be that no one national central bank had a full picture or full powers to call the shots as lender of last resort when they began to implode in the fall of 2008, much less head off the crisis by reigning in the extraordinary levels of risk and leverage they had taken on.

The dominant players in the global financial markets were not just to big to let fail, they were too globally interconnected to let fail.

8

▼

WHAT SHOULD BE DONE?

WHERE WE ARE NOW

The year 2008 will go down in history as the one in which an over-grown and over-mighty global financial system based on high finance collapsed. The scale and spread of this meltdown is without precedent. Never before has finance been so large a part of worldwide economic activity than during the last two decades. We are in uncharted waters. Anyone who says he or she understands what is going on and has a plan to fix it is either a liar or a fool or both. But we all need to try to get a handle on how we got here—there is no good medicine without diagnosis, as Dr. House keeps instructing us on TV—and what the options for treatment really are.

Two basic diagnoses are available to us, given the symptoms we can observe. One is that the patient, the global economy, had a heart attack in late 2008. Therefore, credit for consumers and businesses, which is the lifeblood of the economy, urgently needs to resume flowing.

If we can just restart the heart—the credit markets and the banks through which they pump the blood—then all will be well. Businesses and people will resume borrowing and spending. This will stop the loss of jobs and confidence after a normal, if particularly long and nasty, cyclical recession. So, although the rest of 2009 will be a very uncomfortable year in the ICU with lots of bleeding and vomiting, by sometime in 2010, something like normal bloodflow will be restored and the patient will be on the road to recovery. Economic growth will resume. Perhaps the economy will not be in rude health, but heart attack victims do need to take it easy. This is an optimistic diagnosis because the economic doctors have treated this kind of case before.

These doctors are central bankers, treasury officials, and politicians. They all understand what happened during the last big heart attack—the Great Depression. The patient nearly died then because there was no modern medicine, only superstition. People were dumb back then, we are told. They didn't have computers and Blackberrys. They read books, and worst of all they believed in silly stuff like sound money, low taxes, limited government, and that barbaric relic, the gold standard. In our enlightened age, we are far cleverer. We have the advantage of learning from the mistakes of fools like Herbert Hoover, who nearly killed the patient. Today, we have a big government that can just print money and spend it like crazy, and nice Dr. Bernanke at the Federal Reserve who will, if necessary, drop bales of dollars from helicopters until the patient's heart begins to tick. Perhaps this diagnosis is right. We will all be much happier if it is.

The second diagnosis is really pretty devastating to contemplate. What if instead of a heart attack in an otherwise healthy patient we are dealing with toxic shock in a diseased junkie. Credit has morphed from the lifeblood of the economy into a pathogenic drug in this diagnosis. It has ceased to support healthy functions, real commerce and wealth creation, by being channeled into things that destroy social and economic tissue. If that is the case, then the course of treatment is going to be, by necessity, long and radical. First, the junkie will need to stop taking and depending on the toxic drug. This doesn't mean he will go cold turkey—he is much too sick to survive that—but credit addiction must end over time. Second, once the patient is no longer a credit junkie, a more wholesome form of credit—real healthy blood—will have to be introduced into his system. Again, this cannot be done overnight. But it is vital that the patient gets the right meds in the interim and keeps taking them.

The medicine is likely to be bitter and a bit old fashioned. In fact, all the old stuff about sound money and credit standards that people believed before the New Deal might be essential ingredients. In fact,

maybe the New Deal and all the subsequent wisdom enshrined in the name of John Maynard Keynes (Lord Keynes himself would be horrified by modern Keynesians) started our patient on the road to ruin. Maybe this toxic shock has its roots in the core ideas and institutions of the so-called Progressive Era and of the New Deal itself? If so, detoxification of the patient is going to be tough indeed because these ideas are regaining their power.

Finally, if the toxic shock theory is right, we will all need to get off the stuff, however bad that feels. And we will have to do something to stay off it so we can stop the pushers from coming back into our lives.

Like real heart attacks, the first diagnosis given above makes the patient into a "victim." We can blame stress from work or just bad luck rather than our diet of Big Macs and lack of exercise. The second diagnosis, though, demands that we, like a real junkie, recognize ourselves as the authors of our own destruction. There are no victims. We did it to ourselves. We did it to ourselves by what we wanted to buy and how we paid for it. We did it to ourselves by whom we chose to trust with our money without asking the right questions. We did it to ourselves by whom we voted into office and kept there over the years. So, "it" doesn't need to change, we need to change, and change profoundly, in thought and deed. We need individually and as a society to accept full responsibility for the economic mess we are in, and more importantly, face up to the fact that nobody can save us from our own dumb mistakes.

We are, like Dr. House, forced to act on one theory or other in responding to the financial pathologies that confront us. There is no in between.

It is not the purpose of this book to indulge in a detailed critique of the current efforts of overworked, underpaid, and well-meaning men and women at the Federal Reserve, the FDIC, and the U.S. Treasury—along with their counterparts in other countries trying to cope with the crisis. We will only know in hindsight what worked and what didn't, and even then things will be murky. They always are. People still debate what policies were effective and why during the Great Depression.

However, we are facing a fork in the road as far as broad policies are concerned. If we go down the wrong path based on the wrong diagnosis, the consequences will be severe. Right now, in 2009, there is

still time, barely, to change the course of treatment if we have been mistaken. What does not seem debatable is that when the financial system seized up initially, the patient had to be put into the ICU. Had the authorities not acted to halt the rapid spread of pure blind panic in the fall of 2008 by bold seat-of-the-pants rescues (what the media calls "bailouts") of the large financial institutions, the financial world as we know it might have ended. Or so we are told. The truth will never be established.

Sometimes the greatest act of political courage is to do nothing. Obviously, doing nothing in the face of a market panic would be seen by the voting public as the financial equivalent of the Hurricane Katrina aftermath. No elected official could muster the courage to let the markets clean and cure themselves. As Bagehot instructs us, in a panic, the best thing is to restore market confidence that money will be available to make payments. There is more than one way to do this, however. What Bagehot saw as good practice by the Bank of England and what J.P. Morgan did in 1907 comes down to triage in the ICU. The idea is to find out as quickly as possible which institutions are beyond help and put them out of their misery in a swift, orderly, and humane way. That is why Bagehot advocated a policy of the Bank of England lending freely, essentially without limit, to all players in the market but only upon "good" security—paper that was saleable and intelligible to investors—and at penal rates. Banks without good security and excessive debts would quickly be identified, and those with good assets but a need for ready money would be granted whatever loans they required. Once it was clear that ample money would be forthcoming, the market would place its confidence in those banks that could borrow from the central bank and, above all, in any bank that didn't need to borrow from it. This would reward good behavior on the part of the best-run banks, despite the high-interest penalty they would have to pay for short-term support. In the long run, they would have more business.

The reason we need to provide credit at high, even penal rates, is twofold. First, to make the recipients anxious to get off the central bank's life support system as quickly as market conditions allow. Being a recipient of central bank loans should be as temporary as possible. Therefore, it is wise to make it expensive. Second, by raising the rate of interest prevailing in its market, a central bank would draw in

more money from overseas and from private pools of capital that had been sidelined by fear and uncertainty.

Of course, none of these things have been done in quite this way this time around. When financial markets go south, the first instinct of modern central banks is to slash interest rates, much less raise them. This is the Keynes drill, not the Bagehot prescription. Reducing the cost of borrowing money is thought to be a powerful incentive for people and companies to borrow more and spend more, thus restoring economic growth and confidence. This is more often than not true in a classic business cycle recession or a short, sharp shock to the system like the dot.com stock market collapse or even the aftermath of 9/11. However, this carries a big risk of creating larger problems down the road. Low borrowing costs are an open invitation for people to take risks with OPM. The slashing of rates after the collapse of the NASDAQ tech stocks—a staggering destruction of paper wealth for millions of households—arguably fueled the housing bubble that just burst. The boom in housing that was based on cheap mortgages allowed people to make up their losses in the tech bubble burst that preceded it. So, even when effective, the availability cheap money is always dangerous.

However, sometimes the problem is deeper, and even very cheap money doesn't restore market confidence. Low interest rates are like a string the central bank can use to draw entrepreneurs and investors back into taking the kind of risks that produce jobs and generate wealth. As has often been noted, you can't push on a string. Flooding the market with cheap money is totally ineffective if risks outweigh any obvious opportunities to make money. Cheap money is useless if nobody wants to use it or if those who want to use it no longer *should* have it because of the risk they represent. It is like pumping more and more air into a balloon that has burst. Unless you can find a way to patch it, you are wasting time and energy.

In the current case, the sheer size of the securitized asset mountain heaped up by structural finance makes the efficacy of either the old Bagehot remedy or the Keynesian nostrum of throwing cheap money at it questionable. A lot of ink has been expended trying to suggest that we have seen this movie before and can learn from recent and not-so-recent experience in other countries. We have, in fact, lived through several episodes at the national level of whole banking systems becoming effectively poisoned by bad loans. The root causes are usually real estate booms fueled by plentiful bank loans secured by real estate. Japan is the most extreme case, and we often hear warnings about repeating Japan's mistakes. Sweden also had its banking system go pear shaped in the 1990s due to excessive property lending, except that country is cited as a good example of taking the problem on in an aggressive and effective way. After some initial dithering, the Swedish government took over the two main banks that were clearly insolvent, put their rotten real estate loans into a "bad bank" where they could be worked out over time, put in new management and controls, recapitalized the cleaned-up banks with public and private funds, and floated them on the stock exchange. Within three years, Sweden was returning to growth. The wrong lessons are easily drawn from both these cases though. For example, Sweden's banks had no real international significance, which allowed their problems to be addressed in a purely domestic context. However, these lessons can teach us a thing or two if we use them cautiously.

JAPAN GOES INTO THE TANK

Japan was vulnerable to a banking system collapse because of decades of "industrial policy" in which banks and other key sectors of the economy were over-regulated and financial innovation was stifled by detailed dictates administered by all-powerful government bureaucrats. In fact, it was a model many American politicians admired at the time of our last deep downturn in the 1980s. Japan Inc. supposedly had superior economic performance because politicians, bureaucrats, corporate executives, and unions were all on the same team and decisions were made by social consensus and not by markets. Of course, this way of running things was exactly what Japan and her Axis partners Germany and Italy had embraced in the 1930s, along with the New Deal of America in a far milder form. The results were not entirely encouraging to say the least, but a system in which the government controls the "commanding heights" of the economy retains great appeal to many, notably our current administration.

In the specific case of Japan, this system—often referred to as "corporatism"—achieved wonders in turning a poor and defeated nation into a global economic powerhouse after the war. It largely avoided the pitfalls of a true market economy by strictly limiting the role of financial markets in allocating credit. Instead, very large banks with strong government guidance fed the OPM of millions of thrifty households into large export-oriented industrial groups. These industrial giants had big shareholdings in the banks and vice versa, so bank lending took up the role of bond markets and money markets in America. The big, so-called city banks, rather than the Tokyo Stock Exchange and its regional rivals, decided the long-term survival of Japanese companies. Regulation strictly limited the role of foreign capital and kept Japanese savings invested at home. Regulation also assured bank stability. The bureaucrats at the all-powerful Ministry of Finance (MOF) decided which new financial products were safe, and didn't allow one bank to pursue innovations until other banks could do the same thing. The Japanese themselves called this the "convoy system," where all the ships of finance sailed in formation at the speed of the slowest, with the MOF acting as flagship. Between 1945 and 1997, not a single insured financial institution was allowed to fail.

The result of this government controlled and guided banking system was one of the worst financial bubbles and post-bubble meltdowns ever experienced by an advanced economy. In fact, nearly twenty years after the bubble was popped by the Bank of Japan, the Japanese economy has yet to fully recover. The details of how and why this happened do not concern us here. However, the broad outline of events looks all too familiar from the current American point of view.

First, regulation in Japan limited the kinds of investments that Japanese savings could flow into, especially foreign investments. Increasing prosperity in the 1970s and 1980s did not change the Japanese habit of saving a very large fraction of their incomes. High savings led directly to high stock prices and high real estate prices because the money had to go somewhere within the rigidly regulated Japanese economy.

Second, the banks had never really competed with each other and only lent money based on cozy corporate relationships. There was no need for the five Ps (see Chapter Three). Getting credit outside the Japan Inc. club was a big problem, but inside the club few questions were asked. Loans were based on relationships supported by collateral, especially real estate and corporate stock. As values of both went through the roof, companies were able to borrow more. The banks included stock portfolios in their capital, so they could lend more. The loans allowed companies to buy more real estate, and this drove prices even higher. At one point, on paper, the land in central Tokyo was worth more than the whole state of California.

Third, everybody who was at the top of the food chain—who owned stocks and real estate—felt very rich. In New York, sales people at Tiffany's struggled to learn Japanese. Japanese companies went on a buying binge in an America beaten down by the 1982 recession and the dismal economy of the 1970s. Congress and the pundits predictably went nuts. A minor publishing industry grew up around how U.S. business should embrace Japanese practices.

Fourth . . . poof! The Bank of Japan decided to deflate the bubble by raising interest rates. Suddenly, all the safe, conservative, collateral-backed loans got expensive. Company profits fell. Stocks collapsed. From an all time high of 38,915 on December 29, 1989, the Nikkei average (similar to the Dow) lost half its value in a matter of months. Today at mid-April 2009, it hovers around 8,600. Above all, real estate went into free fall in 1990 and never fully bottomed out.

Thus far, this is a classic bubble, if a very big one, even for the world's second largest economy. Japan's world-beating companies were still selling their products to Europeans and Americans. Japan remained basically a rich country. The problem was there was no Dr. House at the MOF, at least not one to whom anyone would listen. Japan spent the years after the bubble burst in 1990 making a banking crisis into an economic catastrophe. At the time, American bankers, government officials, academics, and other experts told the Japanese they were doing all the wrong things and offered them alternatives. These mainly involved free market solutions for clearing the markets.

Today, we appear hell bent on replicating Japan's mistakes on a vastly larger scale. The obvious need in classic Bagehot terms is to restore confidence in the banking system. This was the case in Japan too, but the extent of bank losses was so shocking that facing the truth was out of the question. Bad real estate loans—property fell 80% to 90% in some areas—perhaps amounted to $1 trillion in a $4 trillion national economy. Nobody really knew how much exactly because buying and selling real estate had simply shut down. Sellers could not afford to eat their losses. Banks had too little capital to admit their potential write-offs. They even lied to the MOF. The whole system was in fact insolvent. Insolvency made it illiquid, of course. Nobody could get a loan. Sound familiar?

The obvious answer was a massive recapitalization of the banking system. Since the Stock Exchanges had plummeted, only public money—from, at the end of the day, the thrifty and hard-working Japanese taxpayer—could do the trick. Here electoral politics reared its ugly head. The Japanese taxpayers were mad as hell and the politicians were terrified of them. Like in our own case, the anger in part stemmed from the grotesque conspicuous consumption and galloping inequality (something Japanese have little tolerance for) of the "bubble economy." Interestingly, during their own real estate driven financial market meltdown, the Swedes did take the problem on directly and spent 20% of GDP nationalizing, recapitalizing, and selling the banks back to the private sector. This was possible precisely because of high levels of public trust in Swedish democratic institutions.

But the Japanese politicians took the one thing that really mattered off the table—bailing out and restructuring the banking system into something useful to the economy. Unlike the Swedes, the Japanese did not trust their politicians. Instead, the government did two things that feel all too familiar. First, they played for time. If the banks were propped up with super-low interest rates—the Bank of Japan got them down to zero and kept them there for a long time—and nobody looked too closely at their books, the real estate and stock markets might come back enough to save them. Sound familiar?

Second, the Japanese politicians went mad on spending and borrowing in the hope of jump starting the real economy. Unlike the "stimulus" that just passed in the United States, which is really vastly expanded welfare and "social" spending rather than spending on public works, the Japanese actually undertook massive infrastructure projects. When they ran out of new roads or bridges to nowhere to build (some of the new bridges were only used by badgers seeking mates), they resorted to paving river beds. These efforts had no meaningful impact on the depressed real economy but were politically useful to the ruling party, which used the stimulus spending to shore up its base of support. Public spending got so out of hand that the government, on several occasion, raised taxes, taking money out of a struggling private economy.

The hope held out by both bureaucrats and politicians was that if the economy could be pumped up with enough public spending, it would grow fast enough for the banks to earn their way out of the hole they were in and for the value of their collateral to recover. However, the government policies failed to do either thing. Bank lending had been central to the economy. Insolvent banks with their books stuffed with worthless loans were the elephant in the living room that nobody wanted to address directly. The banks in turn were propping up large numbers of "zombie" borrowers. Everybody was playing for time.

Time ran out about five years into the post-bubble slump. Small credit cooperatives began to go bust. The old rule under the convoy system was that when a little bank took on water, the government authorities encouraged a large bank to pick it up. Now everybody in banking lacked the means to save other banks through arranged marriages of this sort. The losses on the bride's book were too big to swallow. Japan's deposit insurance scheme didn't have the cash either.

Things got worse. Special housing lenders sponsored by the banks began to sink under growing losses on loans they made to Japanese real estate developers during the bubble. This forced the government's hand. After a fierce debate in the Diet, a bill was passed that, for the first time in history, used taxpayer money to bailout banks. Like the Troubled Asset Relief Program (TARP) plan pushed through Congress at the end of 2008, this bailout caused so much public outrage that politicians dared not even mention further use of public funds to help banks. This made things much harder when main stream banks and securities firms started to fail in 1997. The Bank of Japan could help a bit, largely by lending money to help forced mergers of regional banks. Two major securities houses were allowed to go bust. In November 1997, four banks had failed in one month. People were lining up to take their money out of the banks when the Finance Minister and the Governor of the Bank of Japan jointly promised to protect all deposits.

In February of 1998, the government finally got the gumption to put a huge chunk of public money—the equivalent of $300 billion—into play and set up the Financial Crisis Management Committee to direct its use. No triage of bad and hopeless banks took place. They all got cash injections at the same time, but not enough to make a difference. The Long Term Credit Bank (LTCB) of Japan failed. Attempts at a shotgun wedding failed, and LTCB was eventually nationalized and the rump eventually sold to U.S. investors. The government put in place new laws that set up strong independent bodies that could intervene aggressively, inspect banks, and supervise them. The MOF was taken out of the bank regulation game. Public money was doubled. The RCC (Resolution & Collection Corporation), a powerful body modeled on the U.S. Resolution Trust Corp., was set up to purchase and dispose of bad loans from both failed and solvent banks. An outright banking system collapse was avoided.

YAMATO BANKING

The next thing that happened was less happy for the financial future of Japan. Both the government and the banks themselves decided that the problem had been in part the existence of too many banks. Before the crisis, Japan had ten of the eleven largest banks outside the United States, so her so-called city banks were already huge by any standard. With the blessing of the authorities, Japan's big commercial banks merged into three mega financial groups that dominate finance in the world's second largest economy. These so-called Yamato banks are too large to manage, unable to innovate, and remain very cautious about lending money. Like the 65,000 ton Yamato class super-battleships of World War II, they are just too large to be effective.

Today, Japan is coming to the end of its second lost decade since the bubble burst in 1990. The Nikkei stock average is well below its 1989 level. Economic growth has been anemic at best. The public debt has grown from less than 50% of GDP to 170% of GDP since 1989. Japan's hapless savers make miserable return with 0% interest rates. Japan has remained the richest country in Asia, but it isn't growing, and its population is aging rapidly and actually declining. Despite a few bursts of hope, its economy has more or less come to rest in a semi-permanent state of recession. Yet, the ruling Liberal Democratic Party that presided over this scene hung on to power, largely through patronage and government hand outs, until August of 2009.

LESSON FROM JAPAN

This long excursion into the Japanese financial tragedy of the last two decades is not meant to suggest that the United States is doomed to repeat it. But we seem to have taken a fork in the road that involves repeating many if not most of the same mistakes for essentially similar reasons. These include too much trust in government management of the economy—although the Japanese MOF Mandarins actually did a good job in the post-war decades—and a political fear of using public money to bail out "greedy bankers." In both cases, there has been a strong tendency to deny how bad things really are—especially not to confront the possibility that the whole system is essentially insolvent—in the hope that time and lots of stimulus spending will fix things. There is also the obvious issue of taxing a private economy in crisis more heavily to increase government, and here we risk being far more reckless than even Japan.

CAN WE LEARN?

The great hope for America is that unlike the Japanese we have little patience when we feel we are being had by our government. Basically, like their Japanese counterparts, our political leaders are in effect saying that the key therapy required involves massive government spending and debt increases to shock the patient back to life. It is unlikely that we will give our politicians ten years to try failed cardiac arrest treatments as the Japanese voters effectively did. We will get very angry sooner than that. Yet we need to be careful of cutting off our noses to spite our face.

It is basically childish of us to complain about "bailing out the banks" with "taxpayer money." The deposit money in the banking system belongs to you and me. On December 31, 2007, U.S. banks held $7.3 trillion in customer deposits. Some 60% of these were insured by the Federal Deposit Insurance Corporation, an insurance fund with only about $50 billion in resources to pay back the depositors of failed banks. This is about 1.2 cents on the dollar. Insured deposits almost all belong to households and small businesses, people like us.

If there was a general collapse of the banking system, something that has happened before in other countries like Mexico and Russia and partially happened here in 1930 to 1933, we the taxpayers would be on the hook for at least $4 trillion to give us back our own deposit money. This wouldn't happen. Four trillion dollars is larger than the federal blow-out budget for 2009 and nearly a third of U.S. national income. The government simply doesn't have and probably couldn't get its hands on that kind of money should the current banking crisis go into free fall. The collapse of the payments system based on deposit money would mean no company could pay its bills or its meet payroll. Investors would be wiped out. All our paper wealth and savings would simply evaporate. We would revert to the cash, barter, and private bill of exchange economy that preceded all the real history in Chapter Four. We wouldn't like it, though we might feel that we had gotten even with the greedy bankers.

ROLL THE PRESSES

Of course there is no limit in theory to how much fiat money a government can create through the alchemy of central banking, but at some point flooding the market with dollars will simply destroy its value. This has also happened before, during the 1970s. The Chinese, Japanese, and our other creditors would see their huge holdings of U.S. government debt turn worthless.

Unfortunately, since the Treasury went to a typically clueless Congress last year in the middle of a presidential election, the loaded and phony word "bailout" has been used to inflame passions and score points. As we saw in the Japanese case, fear of public outrage essentially prevented the Bagehot remedy of open-ended use of public money to stop the collapse of the system until things had gotten out of hand. Using too little public money too late made a bad situation worse and ended up costing the taxpayers much more.

The political academic and media elites in America all fear something called "populism," often with good reason. Democratic countries often make lousy economic decisions, such as our opposing free trade and sound money during much of American history. In the long run, however, Ivy League elites are probably much dumber than Joe Six-Pack. As George Orwell once wrote, "There are some things so foolish you have to be an intellectual to believe them." Populist anger with government bailouts and open-ended expansion of government spending and debt may turn out to be our salvation. It may, along with personal revulsion with the cult of debt-driven consumption, drive us towards Plan B, controlled detoxification.

This would be pretty ugly and take a great deal of political courage. That is why harnessing public revulsion is essential to its success. It is not our purpose to lay out a detailed plan. That is way above our pay grade. However, there are some key choices to be made about what kind of financial world we want to come out of this crisis. Among the questions we need to answer are:

First, who should own the banks? Here and in Europe, there are many left-wing politicians who would like to restore themselves to the "commanding heights." This means keeping a large enough stake in the banks to allow credit to become a political goody to be handed out like all other political goodies. The public seems to hate the idea of putting tax dollars into banks or keeping them there. That might prove decisive in preventing long-term government takeover of the financial economy.

Second, how should the banks be governed? Here, public outrage is really only justified when banks that depend on being "too big to fail" push their luck too far. Even among the largest banks, some managed themselves far more responsibly than others. The problem is that many of the largest banks became too large to manage but are too big to let fail. We cannot remain their hostages, however, and the public understands this. Thus far, the handling of the crisis has caused the industry to become *more* consolidated into a few hands. This needs to be halted or reversed by making it expensive to get too big unless you can demonstrate a remarkable degree of control and management skill. The public seems less concerned with the emoluments of very successful bankers—these are no more offensive than those of most top executives—than with the pay practices that allowed the top bankers who wrecked their institutions and the economy come out rich. The public seems to want bad management—as opposed to bad luck—to carry a heavy price.

Third, who should pay for the mess? In any banking crisis, the first order of business is to restore banks' earning power. This often means jerking up fees and interest rates on banks' most vulnerable customers, those who lack financial options. People are outraged over this, as are many opportunists in Congress. Actually, this is really a chance to introduce competition and innovation into the financial services industry, something politicians and heavy-handed regulators can unintentionally kill. Both traditional banks, which do basic banking well—and there are thousands of them—and new innovators like online companies, retailers, and "telcos" can offer the public a better deal. They should be allowed to do so.

Fourth, how do we restore financial discipline? Here, most of the public is not crying out for a bigger safety net as much as they are sick of paying for their feckless neighbors. What is wanted is strict accountability. The real question is, will we look in the mirror and honestly hold ourselves to account? We must see that this is not something that "they" did to us. Demonizing bankers distorts the past and gives no guidance for the future. Everybody should bear the real costs of borrowing too much and lending too much, no matter how painful and damaging it may be to their future prospects. Contracts are central to a market economy and need to be honored and enforced by dispassionate courts, not by Dudley Do-Right judges. The banks are not Snidely Whiplash. They were just being bankers doing what bankers do.

While no prisoners should be taken where fraud is discovered, the truth is that very few men and women working in the banks did anything but their jobs, getting the best possible returns on their shareholders funds given the market they were operating in at the time. Maybe some were greedy, but so were we all, the majority of Americans who directly or indirectly had our savings and pensions in the market. Banks who sat out the whole structured-finance-driven retail credit boom would have lost market value, and their bosses and employees would have gotten the sack.

We would have demanded it. Sitting out a boom is almost impossible for a publicly traded company. The banks misunderstood their real risks and had too much faith in financial rocket science, but even if we resent the enormous salaries and perks they gave themselves, there is scant evidence of illegality or even conscious recklessness related to the collapse. The poster child of the meltdown has become Bernie Madoff, just as Charles Ponzi is still remembered from the Roaring Twenties. Madoff's and other Ponzi schemes by money managers were discovered when the markets plunged, but his scheme was a classic investment scam that had run for decades under the noses of the regulators and had nothing to do with the bankers and instruments at the center of the meltdown. As Warren Buffett wrote, "It is only when the tide goes out that you see who has been swimming naked." We can confidently expect to see a long string of scams and frauds to wash up on the shore.

Within the froth of the bubble, some banks had better controls and risk management skills than others; some were sloppy, and some were tightly run. Some simply had better luck than others. Nobody believed that they were putting their own institutions and careers, much less the whole financial system, in jeopardy. Indeed, the banks and the regulators worldwide believed that financial innovation was leading to a more robust, stable, and safe financial ecology with greater ability to distribute and market risks to those who could bear them. They were all wrong, but they were not crooks. If some bankers behaved badly, many if not most of the politicians now holding show trials and making pompous moral pronouncements about greed bear equal or worse blame for what occurred in the financial markets. We must all accept that the junkie—that is us—really wanted the product.

We need to recognize that the "cops"—the government agencies and the regulators, especially those beholding to the U.S. Congress— were actually putting the squeeze on the bankers to move more product and create more addicts. The Community Reinvestment Act, Congressional and Executive pressure on the GSEs to lower credit standards while blocking effective regulation and oversight of them, and unholy political alliances with "community" groups like ACORN all contributed to the sub-prime mortgage market spinning out of control. The whole politically driven "affordable housing" machinery Congress created from the New Deal onwards created vast and unique distortions in the U.S. mortgage markets that almost cried out for a whole cast of characters from mortgage brokers to house flippers to appraisers to get in on the action and make a buck. Congress defended everyone in the mortgage food chain from scrutiny—after all, they voted back home and made contributions to their campaigns. Main Street banks—so-called regional and community banks— played little role in the current mess and are being unfairly lumped in with the handful of late departed Wall Street structured-finance houses. Every single investment bank has either collapsed, been con- verted into a bank holding company, or acquired by a commercial bank since the summer of 2008.

But the leading financial institutions of Wall Street, the Masters of the Universe, needed no prodding beyond their own titanic arrogance to make what turned out to be some horrible bets. Wall Street got addicted to its own product and died from an overdose. This is really a terrible tragedy for the entire global economy because much, indeed most, of the gains in living standards the world enjoyed since the 1980s was made possible by the American model of finance-driven capitalism.

Politicians meanwhile continue to kick the corpse while denying all responsibility for creating and enabling the bubble that killed the longest period of sustained global economic growth in history.

Conclusion

▼

The one most important thing to take away from this tour of the financial world is that it is not and never can be made safe for anyone. There are tradeoffs in life that we have to make as grown-up individuals and as a society of grown-ups. These have not changed over the centuries. The most basic of these tradeoffs is between liberty and security.

THE MARKET AND LIBERTY

The world of the markets is the world of maximum liberty and minimum security. Markets can make us very rich or very poor for reasons we cannot control or predict. But we can make our own choices about what to do with our own money and at least try to make sure we understand what we are doing.

The American republic was founded as part of a larger project of expanding human liberty called the Enlightenment. The leading thinkers and doers of the Enlightenment, from Adam Smith in Britain to Condorcet in France to Thomas Jefferson in Virginia, were all trying to solve the problem of how to limit arbitrary government power. The European nation state at the time of the American Revolution sought to minutely regulate every trade and every aspect of commerce in favor of specials interests. Guilds, the precursors of trade unions, limited access to trades and set prices on goods that their members produced. Governments everywhere regulated trade and commerce to protect local producers.

THE LIBERAL VISION

Enlightenment thinkers were interested in economic liberty because they knew that it was joined at the hip with political liberty. People without economic choice—that is, choice about how to use their own money and property—would never really have political choice. The real Adam Smith was not so much a free market true believer as he was a clear-eyed observer of life who saw greater threats to liberty and natural rights in the state than in the markets. Businessmen were not good; they were relatively harmless because their single-minded pursuit of wealth actually produced the stuff we needed in our daily lives. The state pursued power and glory, far more dangerous goals. It needed checks on its power.

The U.S. Constitution is the highest example of an Enlightenment project to limit the tendency of all governments to accumulate more power over their citizens. In Europe, this combination of economic liberty and limited government goes by the name of liberalism. The Britain of Walter Bagehot was the epitome of liberal principles in action, with free trade and open financial markets of London its most powerful expression. The United States, despite protectionist tendencies, largely embraced this economic and political liberalism until the so-called Progressive Era took up the idea that the citizen needed to be protected from the market by the state. Big business was seen as and in many cases actually was a threat to both workers and consumers through its power to dominate and rig markets. The state was the only player powerful enough to act as a counterweight to corporate power and greed. Because it was elected by the people, the state was assumed to be an essentially benign actor despite all real history to the contrary.

THE STATE AND SECURITY

The world of the state is the world of maximum security and minimum liberty. States can use their police power over people to seize resources and property from the few and give it to the many. Try not paying your income taxes to see how effective resistance to the engine of confiscation really is. Until the Sixteenth Amendment was passed in 1913, the Constitution effectively limited Congress's ability to impose a national tax on income. In fact, until about a century ago, taxation was almost entirely limited to consumption taxes and customs revenues. Governments everywhere only presumed to tax people's income in time of war and then only people with very high incomes and for limited periods of time.

THE GREAT TEMPTATION

Now it is common for people in places like New York to work half the year and more just to pay taxes. The sovereign moral excuse for this forced taking of people's labor and human capital is a notion of fairness that ignores the skill, effort, and sacrifice required to create wealth. Wealth is just assumed to exist and the government has not only the right but the duty to redistribute it as it sees fit. Fairness requires that government work to reverse the most troubling aspect of the free market: There are always a few winners and many losers, and many of the winners start life on third base. Conveniently, the few cannot defend their property in a system of universal elective franchise where majorities rule, a point that the great Victorian legal scholar A.V. Dicey made in arguing that letting people who got more out of the state than they paid in tax constituted a moral hazard. Politicians would always grab more and more from the few and spend it to buy political power through providing financial security to the many. Representation without taxation leads as certainly to tyranny as taxation without representation.

ILLIBERALISM

The New Deal and FDR's four presidential victories prove that Dicey was on to something, as does the perennial power of socialist parties in European electoral politics. Until quite recently, socialism—which Americans confusingly call "liberalism" or more fashionably "progressive" politics—has had only limited success in the United States compared with other advanced countries like France and Germany. Even the vast expansion of government power and spending that marked the New Deal and the Great Society lacked an explicit socialist blueprint. Socialism—meaning state control of the "commanding heights" of the economy—goes against the individualism of the American character. It is against the grain of our "real history," our Enlightenment political roots, and our healthy skepticism of government power. The collapse of the Soviet Union twenty years ago largely discredited the notion that governments rather than markets should control economic life. The state had clearly failed to deliver prosperity and had destroyed the liberty of billions and the lives of millions in the process. Outside of its strongholds in the universities and cultural elites of the rich capitalist world, state socialism was universally seen to be an abject failure.

THE END OF HISTORY

In 1992, a renowned scholar published a book that stayed on the bestseller list for months. Francis Fukuyama based *The End of History and the Last Man* on a lecture he gave in 1989 when state socialism began to crumble in Eastern Europe. He argued persuasively that "liberal democracy remains [after the fall of communism] the only coherent political aspiration that spans different regions and cultures around the globe. In addition, liberal principles in economics—the "free market"—have spread, and have succeeded in producing unprecedented levels of material prosperity, both in industrially developed countries and in countries that have been part of the impoverished third world." The great debate of modern history between state socialism and liberty had been settled in favor of democracy and the free market economy, argued Fukuyama. How societies and economies should be governed was from now on a closed book. The triumph of Margaret Thatcher in Britain and Ronald Reagan in the United States during the 1980s had started the pendulum of history swinging back to the classical liberalism of Bagehot's Britain. The triumph of the Anglo-American model of business and finance appeared complete and final.

REAL HISTORY DOES NOT END

Of course, real history as we have seen is always a series of accidents. It never really comes to an end. Instead of the end of history, Fukuyama was really observing a turnover in the long, never complete grudge match between free markets and those people and institutions that seek to suppress and manipulate markets through political power. The game continued, and in 2008, the other team—the left wing of the Democratic Party, not its basically mainstream membership as a whole—was able to turn a very scary market panic that had nothing to do with the fundamentals of capitalism into a big score for a return to state control of the economy. Partially, this opportunity was handed to them by the inept Bush administration and events nobody foresaw along with the wretched excesses of bankers and corporate executives that nobody minded when times were good but now suddenly found morally repulsive.

THE ENDURING APPEAL OF THE LEFT

However, the other team, the left, had real strengths that Fukuyama had underestimated. These strengths were largely moral. For one thing, the vision of a benign and wise state promoting social justice and protecting society against the evils of market capitalism never went away. It has always been too attractive a narrative. Sensitive and intelligent people like intellectuals and artists have been drawn to the socialist vision since its earliest days. That is partially why, despite its real-world failures and the horrendous abuses of left-wing regimes, socialism has, from the days of the Popular Front in the 1930s through the New Left in the 1960s and down to today, retained the moral upper hand in the universities and schools as well as the media and culture. Over time, the people in this camp gradually excluded all other points of view from elite cultures worldwide. The anti-globalization and climate change movements as well as the march of the civil rights movement from race to gender to sexuality all gave moral authority to the enemies of the free market and demonized its defenders as bigots and idiots as well as oppressors. Even the Ivy League wiz kids who aspired to become very rich on Wall Street largely embraced this worldview with their money and their votes in the last election.

THE MYTH OF RAMPANT FREE MARKET CAPITALISM

It has been repeatedly asserted by those on the left that the market crisis is the result of policies based on extreme free market capitalist ideology being implemented since the 1980s. This is a myth. In fact, it is fair to say that free market capitalism, red in tooth and claw, far from causing our current crisis, has never really been put into action. The welfare state created in post-war Europe was never significantly rolled back, even in Thatcher's Britain. Even the Reagan revolution at best slowed but never reversed the expansion of the regulatory state. All the major programs and extensions of government power since the New Deal and Great Society have remained in place. Money has remained fiat money. Nobody thought about restoring a link to gold outside of a few economic libertarian purists. The rules and regulations in the Federal Register continued to multiply, along with government programs. U.S. markets remained the most highly regulated by any standard, and litigation by an increasingly aggressive tort lawyer industry imposed ever growing costs on business.

THE RETURN OF THE MARKET

That said, the return of the market, however limited, was very real. The period of 1982 through 2007 saw the return to a joined-up global financial system not seen since the First World War. In fact, prize-winning journalist Tom Friedman of the *New York Times* suggested that the period of state control of the key global economies between 1914 and 1989 was really a long timeout from a much longer trend towards a global market economy. His 2005 bestselling book, *The World Is Flat,* is almost breathless in its description of a world where technology and global finance has integrated billions of producers and consumers into a dynamic global economy. This is a world of incredible advances in human welfare combined with massive insecurity in daily life. Between 1989 and the market meltdown in 2008, over a billion human beings escaped absolute poverty and hundreds of millions more began to enjoy something like middle class prosperity as China, India, and the former Soviet Empire became part of the global market economy. This was the greatest single advance in human material welfare in all of history, largely thanks to global finance capital.

Consumption in rich countries, especially the United States, drove the whole process. The world went to work because Americans went shopping.

TOO GOOD TO LAST

Looking back, the whole thing was too good to be true. The wheels of commerce were spinning on an axle driven by a global money pump. The hundred of millions of new workers in the developing world did not spend their money as much as they saved it. Thrift was hardwired into their way of life because life had always been hard and uncertain. Their countries earned huge amounts of dollars from exports and built up mountains of reserves in their central banks, another sort of savings. This wall of dollars had to be invested in the U.S. markets because only America was big enough, and of course because the dollar was our currency. The newly employed workers of the developing world were in effect lending the U.S. public the money to buy the stuff that workers of the developing world made and shipped to Wal-Mart. It was the Wall Street money pump of asset securitization and structured finance that made this possible, along with the aggressive marketing of credit to one and all by the retail financial services industry. Some rather old-fashioned financial commentators and bankers warned that these "global imbalances" between Asian thrift and American profligacy were going to end in tears for all concerned. These warnings went unheeded because time and again the global financial system based on securities markets proved resilient to shocks. It seemed more robust than the old bank intermediation model. Even the pessimists felt the imbalances caused by America's foreign-financed shopping spree would result in a "hard landing" when things came down to earth. Others felt that the United States and China had in effect become what the historian, Niall Ferguson calls Chimerica, a single economy in which the Chinese made things and saved and Americans bought things and borrowed. Nobody expected a catastrophic global collapse of the entire financial system except a few contrarian economist and commentators like Nouriel Roubini.

When the end did come, what brought down the global economy was not so much the exotic derivatives of the Wall Street super nerds as it was the toxic sub-prime mortgage market born of cheap credit and lax standards. The crime scene had Washington DNA all over the place, from the Federal Reserve Board to the GSEs to their sponsors and protectors in Congress. Politicians of all parties had jumped on the bandwagon of expanding the American dream of home ownership to an ever expanding portion of the population without questioning whether this was really a good idea for the families concerned or the economy as a whole. There is an old British phrase, "safe as houses," to describe why it was prudent to keep money in a building society. You could see and touch these investments.

Real history shows that real estate lending is in fact about as risky a thing as you can do with other people's money. It has been the largest single cause of financial crises over the last forty years, from the U.S. banking crisis of 1974, triggered by collapsing real estate investment trusts, the collapse of the U.S. savings and loan industry in the 1980s, the collapse of the Japanese bubble economy in 1990, the Swedish and Finnish banking crises of the same period, and the Asian banking crisis of 1997. The only response to this inconvenient fact that the U.S. Congress seems capable of is to throw money at the collapsing U.S. housing market instead of simply letting the market clear at prices that attract buyers who can actually afford a house. To protect distressed homeowners, our political masters have felt quite free to violate centuries of contract law and property rights essential to a functioning market economy. There is nothing to stop them from doing so. They have effectively deflected public anger away from themselves and succeeded in demonizing not only the whole financial world but free market capitalism itself. The banking system and financial markets are in the ICU on the government life-support system in almost every major economy, especially the United States and United Kingdom. History has not ended, it has been rewound to the 1970s and before, all the way back to the post-war socialist consensus that lonely voices like Ayn Rand railed against.

YOU AND YOUR MONEY

This brings us back to you and your money. The balance of risk and return in a market can be reasonably gauged when the rules are known. We can't anticipate exactly what the market will do tomorrow, but we can hedge our bets and act on our own risk tolerance. We can make our own decisions like grown-ups and take responsibility for the ones that go wrong. If something sounds too good to be true, it probably is, and those who are not skeptical of the claims of financial professionals can end up at the wrong end of a Ponzi scheme or an exploding interest-only mortgage. However, nobody is compelled to do anything. Markets are about choice.

Political risk is different, as our founding fathers, who knew a lot of real history, well understood. When the state seizes the "commanding heights" of the economy like the banking system and replaces the millions of choices people make in markets with its own superior wisdom, bad things almost always follow. This is not because of bad intentions; good intentions married to arbitrary power can be far worse than transparent malice. This is especially true in a financial crisis when the man and woman on Main Street feel both powerless and angry. They are willing to give those in political power the benefit of the doubt. As the New Deal proves, even failure of strong anti-market policies to improve the economy can succeed politically. The more people find themselves dependent on government, the more they tend to vote for yet more expansion of government. The Depression was worse in 1938 than in 1932, but FDR handily beat Wendell Wilkie in 1940. Whole sections of the United States have become solid, one-party government states after high taxes and regulation gutted their private economies and caused millions of their citizens to leave.

There is a tipping point where those dependent on and employed by government—the "tax eaters"—so outvote the tax payers that formal elections become essentially meaningless. Liberal free-market policies are simply not going to be embraced by the electorate. People who enjoy representation (and government benefits like "free" healthcare) without taxation are only going to vote for more spending and more taxes. We seem to have reached that point as a nation, although it will take a few more election cycles to confirm the trend. When a country reaches that point, the biggest risks to investors become political risks. They are impossible to hedge against.

For example, a "free," government-run healthcare system has to restrict access to and use of new and innovative drug therapies and medical procedures. Anything paid for by someone else develops unchecked demand. Bars would go broke if every night was ladies night. Free healthcare could easily absorb every last dollar of GDP if left unchecked. So the government needs to ration care bureaucratically, for example, denying care to premature infants and older people. It also needs to control the costs of everything it buys, especially medicine. That is why U.S.-developed drugs are cheaper in Canada and Europe. Only in the United States does medical innovation provide positive returns for investors, including the Canadian and European firms that have managed to survive. The U.S. healthcare system drives almost all innovation worldwide because the immensely risky and costly process of medical innovation can pay off here. Put the government in the position of paying everyone's medical bills and you effectively destroy or shrink the value of any stocks that depend on advancing medical innovation.

Subsidize something that the market won't pay for, like so-called renewable energy, and you create value for the shareholders of the favored companies while damaging conventional carbon-based energy firms. And so it goes. Congressional mandates on fuel consumption have had vast and distorting impacts on the economics of the U.S. auto industry. We have seen how government involvement in the banking and housing markets are deeply implicated in the current crisis.

Above all, we have seen this movie before, in the abject failure of socialism and the activist governments of the twentieth century to deliver economic growth and sustained prosperity for their populations.

THE NEW NORMAL

This all matters for you and your money because a political environment actively hostile to capitalism and finance is emerging, what the CEO of the giant bond fund PIMCO, Mohamed El-Erian, calls the "New Normal." As humans, we all depend on pattern recognition. We automatically assume that what has happened in our lifetimes is normal, and any diversion from the straight projection of the past into the future is temporary. We live in the "normal" we have experienced. Unless you are a very old American and remember the economic drift and hopelessness of the 1970s, unless you were out of college and working well before the Thatcher and Reagan revolutions of 1979 and

1980s, you will take the long bull market of the last quarter century for granted. That means that you have to be over fifty to have any appreciation of how bad things can get and how long they can stay bad. There are even a handful of investors still alive who lived through the New Deal. The terrible markets of the 1930s and early 1940s remain part of *their* "normal."

TIME TO BUY . . . OR RUN?

This is not a book of investment advice. However, the reader should by now have come to a judgment about whether we are going through a temporary downturn or a sea of change in the financial world. If the former is true, investors should be taking advantage of beaten-down asset prices to pick up bargains that will pay off handsomely when "normal" conditions return to the market. Most people think this way. People of this view are only looking for signs that the downturn has hit bottom and that signs of recovering are appearing on the horizon. Recovery might take time, but it will come. If, on the other hand, the "new normal" is a world of resurgent state socialism—the polite term is "social democracy"—all bets are off. Capital markets and capital itself are then in for a long hard siege that could last a generation. At the very least, the financial markets might need to weather a lost decade like the New Deal era. If you wait for financial markets to bounce back, you are discounting the political risk, something that real history suggests is always unwise. One radical budget can set a country on the road to serfdom as the Austro-American economist von Hayek dubbed the drift towards democratic socialism. We have just passed such a budget and heard proposed a blueprint for federal government control of healthcare, energy, transportation, including the auto industry, and, above all, the commanding heights of finance. Even at its most radical state, Roosevelt's New Deal was never so audacious about changing the very fabric of American life to suit one man's vision. Elections have consequences.

INDEX

▼

About the Author

KEVIN MELLYN has over 30 years of experience in banking and consulting in London and New York with special emphasis on wholesale financial markets and their supporting technologies and infrastructure. He has been widely published and quoted in financial publications in the U.S., Europe, and Asia including the U.S., European, and Asian editions of the *Wall Street Journal, Les Echos, Fortune,* and the *Nikkei Shimbun* as well as trade publications including the *American Banker, CFO Magazine* (print and online), the *Mercer Management Journal* and the website of the Asian Development Bank. Mellyn is co-author of *X-automating the Firm* (Oliver Lueth Verlag 2002). He holds A.B. and A.M. degrees from Harvard University.